Life Rejuvenated

Getting your mind and life back on track ... after leaving behind expectations and oughtism

ISBN- 978-0-9954398-3-2

re·ju·ve·nate (rĭ-jōō′və-nāt′)
tr.v. re·ju·ve·nat·ed, re·ju·ve·nat·ing, re·ju·ve·nates
1. To restore to youthful vigor or appearance; make young again.
2. To restore to an original or new condition: *rejuvenate an old sofa.*

Philip J Bradbury

I have never read a book quite like this one before. If you're sitting at home feeling that nobody understands you and that despite all your best efforts, you are getting nowhere near finding out what you need to make you happy – let alone being happy – then this book is a must for you. If you have visited countless clairvoyants and sat in circles to try and find your path through life without success, then here, at last, is hard, genuine information to help you make sense of it all.

I identified totally with the author, who explains misconceptions we are ALL brought up with, which have devastating effects on our ability to be happy, whatever we're doing. He takes you on a guided tour of yourself, and explains in simple, easy to read and understand terms, just what you need to do to shake of the burdens that have been imposed on you all through your life, by parents, teachers, peers, and everyone else who has stuck a thumb in the pie that makes up your true being.

I would go as far as to say that in my opinion this book should be required reading!

Jenny Smedley, United Kingdom

కేకేకే కేకేకే

It seems like anyone who is anyone in metaphysical circles these days is writing, or has written, a book. And so has Philip Bradbury. What makes Philip's book different, and a cut above the average, is not that it is based upon his personal experience, or even that he suggests that "we find out who we are by being who we really aren't", but that he provides practical exercises - he shows readers how to apply the insights and techniques that have proved helpful to him and others in their efforts to reclaim their freedom. Philip does this with an astute sense of humour, wisdom and encouragement.

Philip suggests that our primary purpose for being here is to discover who we really are. Most of us are pretty confused about this - we have been programmed to believe that other people know our hearts better than we, and for the sake of being loved by others, we adopt the perceptions they have of us. These perceptions, suggests Philip, are usually based on fear. Self-empowered people cannot be enslaved by fear however, because they know what their own rules are. They know this because they have learned to listen to the whisperings of their own hearts.

Philip suggests that thoughts only affect us emotionally if we choose that they should, and invites readers to observe rather than react to their thoughts. If the thought feels right, thank it, and give it the power of manifestation, i.e., express the thought and act upon it. If not, thank the thought for the opportunity it gave you to make a choice, and allow it to pass. Once we have taken this first brave step, says Philip, the universe will magically step in to synchronise events, people and assistance. At the same time he suggests that we always check our own inner knowing before embarking on the bus to somewhere, especially when someone else is driving.

Philip is refreshingly pragmatic (and accurate) about the meaning of karma. "Handing your power over to a karmic debt system does nothing for your feelings of self-empowerment". Instead, he suggests that we release karmic debt by correcting ourselves and our perceptions. Philip does not lie about the fact these corrections sometimes involve pain, or the shedding of an old skin for a new one. But he is honest about his own challenges, how he dealt with those challenges, what he learned, and how long it took sometimes to make those corrections. It is about allowing, observing and moving through pain rather than resisting. Perhaps one of the most helpful insights he gives, and one that resonated deeply, is that "what other think of you is none of your business - the only thing you have to change is you". In other words, this is your life and your process, so live it.

What Philip offers is practical advice about how to stay on track during the process of empowering ourselves, and he teaches by asking us to ask questions about ourselves and what we really want. If you feel like you are lost, says Philip, you are already on the path to finding out who you are because "admitting you are lost or confused is the first step to becoming found". Continuing on the path means listening to our hearts, and being still until our hearts are moved. In other words: If you're in a rut, stop digging; and, when you don't know what to do, do nothing. Taking our freedom back from our perceptions about who we are, and reclaiming our original intention for being here, is about unclouding our vision. Philip Bradbury's new release "Life Rejuvenated" definitely facilitates this process.

Dr. Michelle L. Crowley, editor of *Talking Total Health* magazine, Clinical Psychologist, South Africa

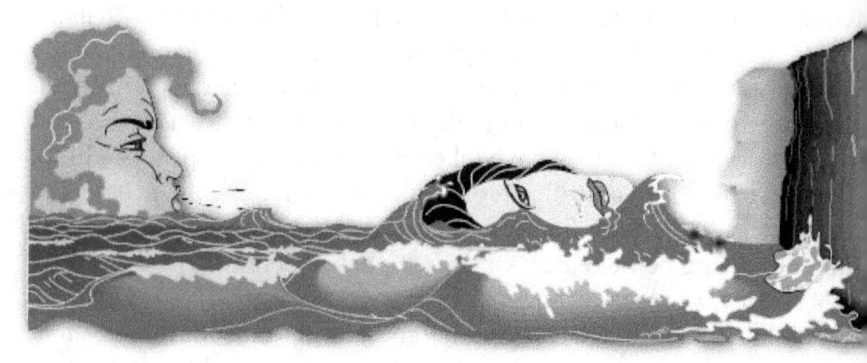

Contents

Why This Book?	6
Teachers And Reminders	8
On Becoming Yourself	*12*
The Phoenix	14
Learning Laziness	16
Unhooking Your Memory	20
The Nature Of Your Mind	23
The Nature of Nothing	30
Activity Versus Action	34
Drinking Deep Of Life	39
The Energy Of Dreams	43
Your Always Knowing	47
Karma (Unedited Version)	54
The Circle Of Life, The Wheel Of Change	59
Practising Your Constant Changes	65
Comfort Zones Or Adventure?	72
Where Did I Leave My Dream?	74
Creating Your Intentional Life	*82*
The Elephant	83
Your Journey	84

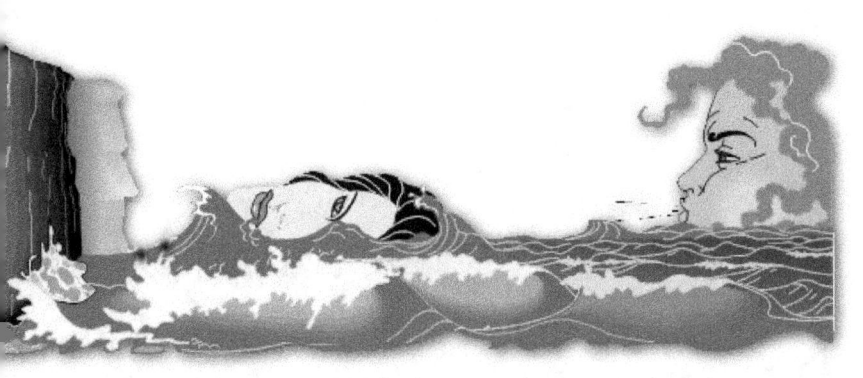

Your Life Purpose	87
The Awareness System	89
Our Life Purpose	93
Learning To Be Me	97
Waking Before You Die	106
Whose Life Is It, Really?	110
Becoming Your Parents	114
Changing Our Water	118
Love Is All There Is	122
Changing Your World	127
Anger And Depression	132
Stepping Out	137
Your Favourite Program - You!	143
Journey Or Destination?	147
The First Big Step	152
My Life In Hell	159
My Life In Heaven	161
Birthday Gift	171
Ideas To Try	173
Philip's Rejuvinated Life	177
About the Author	*180*
Thanks	*181*
More books by Philip J Bradbury	*183*

Why This Book?

Most westerners will spend months, sometimes years, designing their houses – finding the right site, deciding the right size and layout, sourcing the best finance, finding the right architect and builder, choosing the right coloured curtains, the right door knobs, the best toilet seat and thousands of other details – and these westerners will live in their house for an average of five years.

Many people will spend months choosing a car – looking at all the car-yards, reading the motoring reports, getting advice from friends – and the average car will be kept for two years.

Many people investigate computers for months before they buy one and the average one will be kept for a year.

Many people spend over a year planning their wedding and it's all over in a day!

How many people put any time or thought into designing their life, something they'll keep for an average of eighty years? Yet people wonder why their lives are less-than-satisfactory! Many people are happy to design your life for you – your parents, teachers, friends, advertisers, politicians, law-enforcers, bosses, partners, children and, in fact, almost everyone else – and none of their designs will be the same. If you have no input into that, you'll live a life that fits their conflicting expectations and designs, you'll have conflict with yourself and with others and you'll have a life that has nothing of you in it – you'll stop being yourself!

This book may help you change that.

The first part of this book is a story – your story – and it may help you to understand how you've got to where you are now and how you can get to where you want to go.

The second part of the book continues your story and is designed to enable you to become the master and architect of your life. If you read this book and do the exercises, your life will improve – there is no question of that. The amount of improvement is directly related to the commitment and passion with which you do the exercises.

This book will not give you all the answers you need, for those answers are within you. This book will, however, provide a key to the doorway of your own power and beauty. This book will help you discover who you really are and who you've always been but have forgotten for a while. However, we need you to play your part. Together we can create magic in your life! Let's do it!!

Teachers And Reminders

I decided that the best way to learn was to teach. I am passionate about learning about the meaning of life and, in particular, the meaning of my own life and why I'm here. Also, because of the abuse and disempowerment I experienced in my earlier years, I'm passionate about helping myself and others find their own release and empowerment.

I've been running the *Free To Be Me!* courses for many years, in schools and independently, in New Zealand, Australia and South Africa and the ages of participants have ranged from 18 to 78, to date. I'm continually amazed at what I learn about myself as I get to see the world through the eyes, experiences and beliefs of people with such diverse and interesting backgrounds. I am truly humbled by the profound and simple truths from these "ordinary" people and I'm constantly awed by the gold we find as we dig beneath the labels and masks we put on for approval and acceptance. And, as we dig (sometimes gently, sometimes excitedly), people are surprised at the gold they have within themselves – abilities, passions and talents they had forgotten about or never recognised before.

Much of this gold had no commercial value but without it we would all be so much the poorer. As we are able to see inside the depth of one another, we are constantly amazed and humbled at the love, compassion, passion, commitment, strength, softness, tenacity and joy we're able to find.

Just as participants' backgrounds and experiences are diverse, so are their reasons for attending the courses. Some of the reasons people come are to:
- Start a business importing Spanish horses,
- Find ways of improving their relationship with their mother,

- Learn how to say "No", and to say it without guilt,
- Find their passion or reason for being here in this lifetime,
- Learn how to create space and time for themselves,
- Learn the reason for their anger and how to transform that energy into something more positive,
- Be more courageous in taking business risks,
- Learn how to smile each day (one lady had been unable to smile for the previous three years),
- Find more meaningful work,
- Learn how to be a good friend and how to attract good friends,
- Learn how to be more confident in groups,
- Have more fun.

The reasons are limitless and I, of course, don't have all of the answers. Actually, I don't have any of the answers and as a teacher I'm aware that the word education comes from the Latin *educere*, which means to draw out ... to draw out that which is already there but we've forgotten. Actually, I'm more of a reminder than a teacher and the process of the course is designed to allow people to find their own answers, their own truth.

Because we've all been so thoroughly trained to believe that anything and everything we need has to come from someone else, some participants will resist that for a time ... and then I experience a poignant and fulfilling moment when a smile comes over their face as they realise that they do indeed know who they are, do know what they want, do know what is best for them and do know what they're here for. And these smiles of realisation are often accompanied by tears, leaps of joy and/or huge sighs of relief. So trapped are we in the belief that all our solutions (and hence our problems) must come from others that it can be a traumatic and freeing step to move beyond that belief. Beliefs are like sunglasses and while we all recognise that they colour the way we see the world, we often forget that we can easily take them off.

I continually forget as well: Recently, a participant wanted to know what else she could do to accelerate her growing psychic and intuitive abilities. I was about to give her a list of the groups and individuals she could go to when my inner voice boomed in my head, "Nothing! Do nothing." A bit nonplussed, I asked for clarity and in the split-second that these inner conversations take, a different way occurred to me. I opened my mouth to speak – it was not about doing extra things but about doing no-things. I explained that her intuition was intuition from inside – her inner knowing. If she was going to rush off to another spiritual development group she would be getting outtuition, which was the opposite of what she was looking for. My suggestion and our discussion centred around ways of finding space in her busy life to be totally alone with herself and to be totally absorbed in herself, whether that be in an activity that she was passionate about or actually doing nothing – day-dreaming, counting clouds or meditating. We both remembered together!

Our constant training has been that to be a better person is to continually add to that which we are – learn skills, obtain qualifications, acquire assets, add make-up, have new experiences, learn new behaviours – and suddenly, we realise there has been so much plastered to our simple, beautiful and powerful essence that we started with, that we've lost sight of it. Our first impulse (due to our training) may be to learn what or who we are from someone else and so we slap on another layer of plaster. So we see even less of ourselves and then we learn a new skill or behaviour and the beauty and power of our true essence is hidden even deeper beneath the layers of others' truths. Then somewhere, sometime, somehow, we say, angrily, sadly, despairingly, "ENOUGH! I want me back!"

Though we may not feel it in that moment, we're finally on our way. If we pretend we're O.K. when we're not, we'll stay in not-O.K. The best first step to finding ourselves is to say, "I'm lost." To say, "I'm frightened" is the best first step to releasing fear. To say "I'm angry" or I'm depressed" is the best first step in moving away from anger or depression. In the moment of our greatest frailty and vulnerability is the opportunity for our greatest strength and beauty to arise, if we can admit to that frailty and vulnerability. As our phoenix rises from the ashes, we realise that the best course to take is to begin unlearning, to start peeling off the plaster and to get back to the strength and beauty that we really are.

It doesn't matter how psychic, caring, insightful or close other people are, no one knows what you really need as well as you do. No one has your family and your body and your experiences and your dreams and your beliefs. You are unique and on the subject of you, you are the complete answer, the most qualified expert and no one else knows your truth as well as you do. At times you may need others to remind, encourage and nurture you but, in the end, the only truth is that which you are.

We cannot clean our water and windscreens by adding things – they only become cleaner, clearer and more effective by subtraction or by taking away the impurities. So it is with us and as we become more free to be who we really are, we experience greater joy, peace and fulfilment, and only then can we really make a positive difference in this world.

I thank you for allowing me to write this for I often forget – you have allowed me to remind myself of my truth … what a brilliant teacher you've become!

On Becoming Yourself

The secret of life is to know that there are no secrets. To become a better person, a saintly being or a great and wise master, you need to know that there is nothing for you to do. You are already all those things. There is absolutely nothing to do, except that which you feel passionate about, that which stirs your heart, that which you feel good about in every given moment.

"But!" you exclaim with exasperation, "How do I find out what my passion is?"

A good question for, if you are a normal, average human being, you will have grown up with a head-full of rules, expectations and beliefs that tell you what you should be doing and what you should feel good about. Somehow, one day, you will feel the need to peel away those layers of rules and that, my dear reader, is the only purpose you have in being here, on this Earth – to know thyself. There is nothing else to do.

You were not born in sin and you have no karmic debts. Those who would tell you those things are those who give you a lot of rules to follow – their rules. They are very frightened people who have a need to keep you chained to their beliefs for, in their insecurity, they fear to walk their path alone. They have yet to know who they are and feel a need to do that through you. That does not work and you will be doing them (and yourself) a great favour by thanking them and walking on by .

You are absolutely perfect as you are, and you have always been that way – perfect. Absolutely perfect. You do not need to do anyone else's *Ten Steps to Heaven* or *Twelve Steps to Enlightenment*, or become vegetarian, celibate, beautiful, educated, reclusive, charitable or noble. You are as you are as you are and you need not be any other way. Neither stars nor numbers nor anything else controls your life – you are in charge. You are a wise and powerful being and your simple mission is to realize that wisdom and that power. You are to realize those things by learning to express them. You are not meant to be expressing your power in a positive way – you are simply meant to be expressing it in *your* way. If you are frightened of it (and yourself) you may harm others. Through that you will learn not to harm others. You will then find respect and loving for yourself and, from that place, you will only be able to do good. You will have no other choice and you will want no other choice.

This book is not a truth. It will not help you become enlightened or better. It makes no such promises for it cannot make such promises. This book is simply a collection of words that form part of a philosophy, a philosophy that is being continued in further books. It is not a truth. I invite you to read my philosophy but please bear in mind that that is all it is. For it to become a truth is for you to experience the philosophy, to see it work in your miraculous life. Only then does the philosophy become a truth. Only then do you realize your truth. Only then do you become your truth.

Only then do you become yourself.

The Phoenix

To rise above your station,
Takes a brave heart,
A pure soul,
And a willingness to play your part.

To rise to a different level,
Means you leave behind a few.
They'll be sad or jealous,
And wonder what's got into you.

The ones you leave behind,
Aren't forgotten or loved any less.
You see them less but love them more,
But they can't understand, or even guess.

Take the next step with joy, Dear One,
For each step forward gives new friends -
Quieter, stronger and more like you.
Their quality and friendship never ends.

So hold to your strong heart,
Your beautiful soul and smiling eyes.
You deserve the best of all there is,
Having more "hellos" than "goodbyes".

Learning Laziness

The hardest and best thing we can learn is to learn how to unlearn all the learning we've learned – in the emptiness of knowledge is who we really are.

This is a book for lazy people – extraordinarily lazy people – who want to realize the greatest potential they have within. I do not say this to entice you to read further, for being lazy is probably the most difficult thing you will ever have to do. And, you will find, being lazy is the best way to achieve the most you are capable of. Confused? Concerned about my sanity? Good, for if you aren't, you have no business reading this book – you must already be an extraordinarily lazy person and, therefore, an extraordinary human.

For most of us, the constant urge is to be forever busy, forever thinking, forever planning, forever being unlazy. Much of this has come from being constantly encouraged from childhood:

Learn to smile (clap, clap!)
Learn to walk (clap, clap!)
Learn to talk (clap, clap!)
Learn to tie shoe laces (clap, clap!)
Do your school work (clap, clap!)
Practise your sport (clap, clap!)
Learn hard at your trade (clap, clap!)
Learn hard at your profession (clap, clap!)
Be a perfect home-maker (clap, clap!)
Work hard at your looks (clap, clap!)
Get married (clap, clap!)
Have children (clap, clap!)

Bring them up "correctly" (clap, clap!)
Abide by the rules (tax laws, traffic laws, criminal laws, family expectations, society expectations, moral laws, etc,) (clap, clap!)
Buy a nice house (clap, clap!)
Have a good job (clap, clap!)
Have a steady income (clap, clap!)
And on and on and on …
There is so much we have to achieve …

Every time we do something well, we are applauded and this helps our feeling of goodness about ourselves – our self-esteem. And so we learned from day one, with millions of reminders, that if we want to feel good we should do something that's in line with our family or society expectations. We will then get noticed, we'll get clapped and then we'll feel great about ourselves. Yet another buzz. Yet another high. And so we live in constant need of applause and get it by being unlazy.

How many people do you meet who tell you how busy they have been? Most people? It's really cool to be seen to be busy – busyness (business?) is created to get another round of applause. The less you believe in yourself, the quicker your esteem tanks run out and the more they need refilling with applause – you then create more busyness (real or apparent), tell everyone about it, get many claps and then feel great about yourself for another short space of time.

The sad thing is that if you feel you cannot create or do the things society and family seem to expect, you become a "loser" in some way. If you do not:
Pass all your exams (naughty child)
Excel at sport (naughty child)
Look like beautiful people (naughty child)
Have a wonderful job (naughty child)
Have a job (naughty child)
Have a conventional job (naughty child)
Have a well-paying job (naughty child)
Raise children "correctly" (naughty child)
Marry the right person (naughty child)
Stay married (naughty child)
Act grown-up and sensibly (naughty child)
Follow the rules (naughty child),
And on and on and on …

You are scolded in the appropriate manner by yourself and others. This scolding so often ends in depression, addictions, violence and/or suicide.

These scoldings happen many more times than does the applause (usually, the first word a child learns is "no" as that's the word they hear the most) and if you're not motivated by the clapping, you're well and truly motivated by the scoldings.

Because the applause and scoldings started at a time when we had no conception of ourselves, no other knowing except what came from the outside, we absorbed them like a sponge and they became us. Because these big people supplied all our needs, we quickly began to believe what they said, did and thought. Whether they were expressed or not, we knew very well what these beliefs and expectations were. They became a part of us so thoroughly that when we started thinking for ourselves as children or, later, as self-sufficient adults, we automatically applauded or scolded ourselves (based on the expectations we carried within) as the "big people" did to us. In fact, when we did anything wrong, it didn't matter what others said about us – there was no greater critic than ourselves. And so we became parents to ourselves – very harsh parents. I still hear older people saying things like, "Oh, I know what my mother/father would have said about that!" Their mother or father has long since died but their rules and judgements live forever, in each succeeding generation, if they choose to allow it.

So, when I ask you to be lazy and you find this very difficult, you may now understand why. If you attempt to follow my laziness ideas, even for split-seconds, you may observe your parent-self scolding or beating up (mentally) your child-self. If you do, then well done, and welcome to the human race. Or, should I say, you will be doing what over 90% of other humans do. It's O.K. to beat up on yourself for being lazy or even contemplating laziness. Yes, it's perfectly O.K. to do that!

What I would strongly suggest is that you don't beat yourself up for beating yourself up for being lazy. That may happen. Instead, simply observe your parent-self and watch how it reacts when you contemplate certain courses of action or inaction.

We will, later, be developing ways of allowing ourselves to do things that are right for us, though they are in conflict with our "training" or with family or society rules. This is a major shift in thinking and attitude, however, and cannot come about without learning some acceptance and compassion for ourselves. Our "Silent Witness" will help that acceptance and compassion to grow and we will get to know hir[1] soon. It's O.K. to be impatient (you're allowed to beat yourself up for it!) and want to know this right now, for impatience is partly what's driving you to make these positive changes – that's great! However, in the meantime, you may like to ask your beautiful guide of patience to be at your side, for in stepping slower, we step steadier and don't have to back-track.

This laziness I talk of is not the laziness of the body but of the mind.

So many people are told that they are lazy – especially those who do not "make it" in the job-finding scene. This makes it harder to keep the esteem tank full, to be confident in interviews, to get jobs and to hear more "lazy" accusations – a spiral that's hard to break out of. You are not lazy, you have never been lazy and you will never be lazy. There are no lazy humans. There are many people who have not found what it is that stirs them and there are many people who know what it is that stirs them but are not yet doing it, for whatever reason – most people are in one of these two categories. You, too, may be like these people and, because of it, may be without:

A job,

A partner,

Friends,

Self-esteem, and/or

Inner contentment, but how can you be lazy when you're reading a book to improve yourself? You aren't lazy and you can stop beating yourself up for it, if you like. As a human it is almost impossible to be lazy for two reasons:

As explained previously, we are trained, from birth, not to be, and our very natural selves (trained or not) are built to be very unlazy – or very busy.

What are you doing at this moment – fiddling with a pen, stroking this page, playing with your hair, wiggling your leg, tapping your foot, picking your nose, humming a tune or moving some other body-part that doesn't need to be moved?

As with your body, so with your mind.

---

1 Used to denote either him or her.

Philip J Bradbury

Unhooking Your Memory

Conscious forgetfulness is the most effective way to remember anything.

In order to get the most out of the words in this book, it is best to read and forget them. If you remember them, you forget yourself and this book is about helping you to remember who you are[2] – you can't do that if you are constantly trying to remember who I am.

Let's do a simple exercise and you will see what I mean:

Just sit quite still and shake your head a little. Can you hear it? No? Shake a little harder and listen for a tinkle or rattle. Hear it? No? Shake a little harder and longer and ... yes? You can hear it! Great! The bone marrow in your spine constantly manufactures little hooks which it then wraps in a very thin, soft and strong plastic (so they don't stick on the way up) and then sends them up to a special depository at the base of your brain. As you shake your head you will, occasionally, hear these mind-hooks rattling.

Now, as you know, your original and true memory is stored just behind your heart but your mind (busy and helpful little thing that it is) does not like to be outdone and has created a back-up system. Part of the mind's system is these little mind-hooks, which it contracts the bone marrow to manufacture for it. When a thought passes, a hook will fly out and grab it, putting it in a holding-bay near the mind-hooks. That's how the mind's memory works. It is a fairly basic system (copies are never as good as the original) and works reasonably well, but has a few drawbacks:

1) Negative thoughts are always rougher, softer and irregular – easy

---

2 See the chapter, *Karma - the Unedited Version*.

for the hooks to grab. They are never missed. Positive thoughts are harder, smoother and round and get easily missed by the hooks.

2) As the hooks are barbed, they cannot let go of thoughts once they are hooked and stored – they stay with you forever. That is good as you never forget how to tie your shoe laces, ride your bike or to say "please". But, if new thoughts come along that contradict previously hooked ones, the hooks invariably miss – almost as if they didn't pass by at all. Opposing thoughts cannot be held together in the same brain.

3) Each thought hooked into your mind becomes your master, and confusion (as well as headaches and migraines) reigns as different masters are snared.

4) If the mind is not connected to the heart (as in most people) it has no perception of what the heart needs to be fed with, and simply grabs at everything that passes. This results in the mind becoming full of thoughts that are inappropriate, incompatible or useless for that person. As the pile of thoughts grows and grows, in the thought-bay, it becomes harder and harder to see past it to the needs of the heart. A person then becomes the stored thoughts (appropriate or otherwise) which is, inevitably, a move away from the true heart or knowing of that person – confusion, mental illness and lack of self-knowing follow.

An example of this is often seen with people getting into this "New Age" stuff. They are swamped by wonderful new ideas and activities and the mind-hooks become extra busy, grabbing each new thing as it passes. First there are astrology books and lectures, then it's off for a psychic reading, then a channelling, then some Ascension exercises, then some Yoga exercises, then watching for U.F.O.s, then studying the Mayan calendar, then it's on to crystals and then the Hopi prophecies, then Buddhism, Taoism and vegetarianism, then Tantra and then hypnosis … with the body and mind flying all over the place with no sense of direction or discernment. And, after all of that rushing around, "out there", where is that person? They are everywhere and nowhere, trying to serve many masters and never serving themselves, not "in here". They are lost, living not their dream but the dream of their well-meaning friends who insist they do this, that and the next thing. They have to live the dreams of others for they've lost their own.

There is nothing to learn – the only purpose we have here is to remember who we are. If partaking of any of the above New Age activities helps, that's great, but you can become a higher spiritual being by doing none of the so-called "spiritual" things. Just be, and remember.

So, what to do with all these hooks? You can't throw them out[3] so just allow them to have a rest. Now, close your eyes and relax for a while. As you relax your body, you will feel your brain relaxing as well. As this happens it will feel as if the atoms in your brain are coming apart from each other, very slightly – tiny spaces are happening between each atom, each cell. You can feel more space in your brain and it feels really light and quite pleasant. Now, as you read these words 99% of them are going in and out of your brain, straight through the little pathways of space you have allowed to be there. Everything goes in and everything goes out again. Nothing stays. Every now and then, a thought will quietly slip down through the spaces and land in behind your heart – you will feel a little "clunk" or "aah" as it softly lands.

You will know if your new "spaced-out system" is working at any time for, after reading something or listening to a speaker, you will not remember one fact. You may not even remember who the author or speaker was or what it was all about. In time you might even forget your own name and where you live, but that sort of progress can only come when you become totally adept at thought-less living.

What you will find, however, is that you become more aware of yourself – as you observe the little knowings that sneak through the tiny holes, your heart will go "aah!" more often, and grow. You will also find that you have total recall of the essence (what it was really about) of everything you learn – unclouded by facts. And, curiously, the facts you need will just be there. You may not recall the facts immediately after you leave the lecture or put the book down, but they will be there, later on, when you need them.

In this way your heart draws in what it needs and the rest is gone, with you staying totally in control and your sense of self entirely intact. You now have all you need – yourself.

I dare you to try it.

---

[3] See the chapter, *The Nature of Nothing*.

The Nature Of Your Mind

Your mind is the container in which your life is formed.

It has been said that we think five hundred thoughts a minute and then we're told we're lazy thinkers! We don't even have to think about thinking at all, and we're still doing it at five hundred per minute! I guess we all have different definitions of lazy.

So, If we're naturally busy beings, why am I asking you to become something against your very nature, something you cannot help being, something lazy?

I could get you to feel really horrible by asking where has your super-active brain got you to date, but I won't! Let us just pretend that you have tried all the "other" ways, the logical ways of trying to get what you want – dreaming, setting targets, doing budgets, talking to your God, doing visualisations and the many other things you can do. Let us also pretend that you still do not have what you really want or, quite likely, you do not even know what it is that you want, to then know how you're going to go about getting it. Let us also pretend that some inner urging is now asking you to try something quite different, quite illogical, quite against all your former "training", quite stupid, for little else has worked. Let us also pretend one more thing – that that inner urging has led you to this book. If the way this book came into your life was without any great effort, in a magical or unusual sort of way and the stuff in it works, we could pretend that all other worthwhile attainments could be effortless – i.e. done lazily. This is just a theory, at the moment, and we can test it out later.

Before we find out how to get things, it may be helpful to ponder on the thing that gets us those things and, hence, consider some things

about the nature of our mind:
- Is it a thing or a process?
- Are we our thoughts?
- Do our thoughts come from us?

Before we do that, I just want to clear up one little matter – that of our brain! Many people study the brain in order to better know our thinking process. I'm not sure that that's very helpful and I ask all you car drivers – "How many of you know how a car's motor works? Do you need to know that before you can drive from A to B in a car?" Obviously not. The same applies to the understanding of our thought processes – that the motor goes is not in doubt. The only limiting factor now is the driver's ability to drive and knowledge of where to go. What we really need to know is how the driver directs the car and how s/he knows how and where to go – you are the driver and your brain is the motor. We will concentrate on the driver.

Your mind – how can you lose it?

People often ask how they can have peace of mind, or how they can have a peaceful mind. The answer is that it is not possible – there is no such thing as a peaceful mind. The only thing that is peaceful is the state of no-mind, the mind that is without thoughts.

Ponder on this for a moment:

You are observing a crowd of people on a street corner. What is that crowd? Is it a thing or a process? If half of the people leave, will there still be a crowd? If another half of that leave will it still be a crowd? If all leave, except one person, is it still a crowd? So what constitutes a crowd – 2, 3, 10, 20 people? And when all the people leave, where will the crowd go?

Obviously, the crowd went nowhere because it does not exist. It is not a thing, it is a process, made up of the gathering of a number of people.

So it is with our mind – it is like the crowd and only exists by virtue of the thoughts that flow through it. If we have no thoughts, where has our mind gone? The answer is that our mind has gone nowhere for it never existed in the first place – it was never a thing. Our mind is nothing but a collection of thoughts and when they go, it ceases to exist. Now, you may ask, what is the point of pondering on the mind when it doesn't really exist? Good question and the answer is that there is no point.

The important things to ponder on are thoughts – the things that make up the mind.

With five hundred a minute, there can't be many spaces between thoughts and so it's easy to see how we can imagine that our minds are something substantive – one huge congealed mass of connected thoughts, with no spaces between. However, if we can think of our mind as individual thoughts (which it is), it's easier to imagine that there could be spaces between them. For most people, the spaces are so small as to be unnoticeable. It is possible, though, to observe the spaces and, as we do, to create larger spaces between each thought. It is very helpful to do this as each space is what I call our God-space. Between each thought (which is our output to the universe) is a space which is the input from the universe. Whether we call this our intuition, gut feelings, subconscious, super-consciousness, higher-self, God-space or whatever, it is the source of our greater knowing, the place from which we get those ideas and things that we "just know". If we can increase the space between each thought then we have more access to that place of our greater knowing.

If you can increase the spaces between the busy thoughts, you will experience two benefits:

With less thoughts comes more peace.

With more spaces, comes more knowing.

We will come back to those spaces later and, in the meantime, let's look at how our thoughts can affect us.

Who's boss, you or your thoughts?

You are looking at your television screen. Before you turned it on, it was a clean and blank screen. Now, with the television on, you see a continuous flow of images on the screen. These images are constantly moving before your eyes and appear (to your eyes) to be the screen – as distinct from on the screen. You see people, animals, buildings, cartoons, multitudes of colour and design and they all seem to be in the screen. You now turn the television off and where have they gone? The screen is clean and blank again. None of the colour or shapes have been left behind on the screen – all have completely disappeared. You cannot see the images without the screen, but the screen is not the images and remains nothing more than a screen – totally unaffected by the images it allows you to see. The images pass by it, you observe them and they are gone.

So it is with your thought-screen, your brain. Without your brain you are unable to sense thoughts but your thoughts are not your brain or any other part of you. They pass through and your brain is not changed or affected in any way. This is the way of the Silent Witness – simply observing the thoughts that pass through and allowing them to disappear as the images do from your television.

Thoughts only affect us emotionally if we choose that they should. As they pass through, we choose whether to observe and let them pass, or to hold on to them and allow them to affect our emotions. It is our choice, though we may not be aware of the choices we have been making – up till now.

Have you ever noticed how one incident can affect different people in different ways? Say, a news item, which some people may get really angry about and others merely shrug and say "so what!" The same fact or event – different levels of attachment to it. You can choose your own level of attachment to every thought (all five hundred a minute!) that passes through.

You can become the Silent Witness to your own thought processes, simply observing the thoughts as they pass through. It's a fun game to play, to allow strongly emotional thoughts (ones of anger, passion, sadness, exhilaration) to pass through the lens of your mind (your brain) and allow them to pass out again, without any attachment. Simply observing.

With this knowing you can now take greater charge of your thoughts, emotions and life. However, just because you now know something new and really powerful, please do not beat yourself up if thoughts and emotions still buffet you around for a while. Having a head (intellectual) knowing of something is not the same as having a heart (experiential) knowing and it may take some time and practice for the knowing to become a natural part of your being. In the same way that you stumbled many times before you walked, you will probably get attached to things you wish you hadn't. That's O.K. Just keep observing, keep practising and, in time, it will become easier and more natural.

It is said that attachment to the past isn't helpful and this is largely true, but the past can become a good friend. To see your progress, remember where you were, not where you're going. The journey is never over and you are always able to beat yourself up for not being there – wherever "there" is. Look back, see where you've moved from, smile and know you're progressing well.

Now, you may ask, what is this attachment? How do we attach to things? You may feel you need to know this before you can then know how not to attach – you don't[4] but attachment is created by judgement. Each time you see a thought and then try to put it into some judgemental category (good, better, bad, disgusting, brilliant etc.) you attach to the thought and it becomes your master. Simply observe. Don't even try to cease judgement, simply observe. It is not possible to stop thinking negative things – it is only possible to think positive things, as you will see later on. Negative thoughts are no-thoughts – simply an absence of positive thoughts. So, simply observe. Observe yourself observing. Observe yourself reacting. Observe and smile.

Who thinks your thoughts?

So if thoughts just pass through from somewhere to somewhere else, where do we come in? Don't we think them up, by ourselves? Sorry, but no. Not one thought that you have ever had has ever come from you, in the same way that not one image on your television screen has ever come from it. All thoughts are foreigners – they come from somewhere else.

The universe is one huge thought, composed of the thought-children it spawned, which spawned further thought-children and so on. The thoughts that pass through you may be great-great-great grandchildren of the Original Thought or parents of the thought you had just before. Many thoughts have been made manifest by the creative power we have and so here we stand, manifested thought – as do all planets, buildings, animals, hamburgers and toilet-rolls.

Our sacred mission is to be a conscious television screen for all thoughts and, with discretion, take those that are right for us and to bring them to realization, to manifestation. Everything that can be thought, can be done – everything is possible.

So, rather than beating yourself up for thinking "evil" or "negative" thoughts, you now know that they aren't even your thoughts. Each thought is, in fact, an opportunity which you can choose to follow up on or to let go of. So just observe each thought as it passes through and

---

4   See the chapter, *The Nature of Nothing*.

make your choice:

If it feels right, thank it and give it the power of manifestation[5].

If it doesn't make your heart sing, thank it for the opportunity it gave you and allow it to pass on.

Belief and doubt - brother and sister

Belief and doubt are different sides of the same coin – they are the same thing reversed. If you believe in something, you have to exert mental effort to hold to that belief. Everything you see or hear that coincides with that belief is yet another confirmation that you are right and so you collect and remember that new thing. Everything you see or hear that contradicts your stance, has you finding more facts to prove the rightness of your belief. It is important that you continue to prove your belief to yourself and to others, for when you are sitting on belief, it's a flat and slippery seat that you have to continually cling to.

Doubt involves the same mental effort and each new reality you are presented with has you working hard on claiming (possessing?) or denying that truth, and having others share your doubt.

Both require constant mental effort.

The easy (lazy) way is the way of knowing, the comfortable armchair of truth you sink into. There is no mental effort involved for it has nothing to do with your mental faculties. Knowing simply is, and its truth for you sings through your heart, not your head. In knowing, you do not possess or reject – you simply know. No need for proof, no need for justification, no need for anything. It just is (justice?) or it just isn't – end of story. And, because there has been no possession or rejection, it means there is no effort involved when your inner essence, your beingness, alters. You can simply move without taking any baggage. The lazy person's way to move house.

Observational changes

It's a strange thing, this thought thinking, this pondering on the real nature of our mind, for, it seems, the less work we do, the more it works for us – yet another of life's contradictions.

The less effort we put into attaching to our thoughts, the greater peace and control we have in our lives. You will also notice four other things:

---

5 See the chapter, *The Energy of Dreams*.

The first is that the more observation you do, the more you can do and the more you want to. The insights and contentment that come from playing the role of Silent Witness to yourself are such that (like sex, eating and other pleasurable pursuits) as you do it, you will want to do it more often and for longer. And, similarly, the more you do it, the better you get at it.

The second thing is that your first observations may have been of a constant stream of thoughts, day and night, with no spaces between. However, as you continue to simply observe (without attachment or judgement), the separate thoughts become more distinct and the spaces between them larger. You may even find you have seconds or even whole minutes with no thoughts floating through at all. And, as you observe this, you don't get excited or sad – you simply observe with a simple knowing that things are changing. There is nowhere to go, nothing to achieve, nothing to gain or lose – changes are observed and an inner peace and contentment expands within your being.

The third thing is that, as you simply observe, without attaching any judgements to the thoughts that pass through, more and more will be congruent with your true self. As time passes, you will observe that less and less of the thoughts are able to be judged as "wrong" or "negative". As you allow the process, you also allow your true self to shine through – so more "right" thoughts come into your mind and more "right" things come into your life. It just happens as you allow it, effortlessly.

The fourth thing is that, at first, you are able to stay in observation for very short periods of time (for seconds or less) but as you continue to observe, you can watch for longer periods of time. Not only do you do this because it is so enjoyable (consciously), but you start to do it unconsciously, automatically, as your unconscious mind loves it so much. As you allow it, the Silent Witness does hir job, without you having to tell hir to do it.

Laziness becomes effortless.

The Nature of Nothing

If we give a "nothing" a name, we immediately create the illusion that it is a "something", something to battle with.

They may tell you to get rid of your bad habits but how can you get rid of that which isn't there? "Banish evil thoughts from your mind", they say, but how can you banish something that's not in there?

Getting hooked

The human mind or "thought receptor" (for want of a better term) has great trouble visualising or conceiving anything not previously experienced. The mind likes to hook new ideas or experiences onto previous ones, to give a frame of reference and some security. New ideas can feel quite scary so we throw out an anchor, or hook, to secure us to the safety of previous and known experiences and ideas.

This "hooking" is something we are very good at – if we know someone at school called Michael and he was, say, an absolute pain, we remember that and the next few Michaels we encounter are immediately tarred with an "absolute pain" brush. Often this is how we choose our children's names – we use the names of people we like and not the names of those we don't like. Past experience creates future experience. If we had a, say, Ford car that went really well, we might stick to always buying Fords in the future – all Fords are great because one was. If our first Ford was always breaking down, we may never buy another one, saying to ourselves and others that all Fords are hopeless cars – all Fords break down because one did.

When a new experience comes along, we immediately look for a previous experience to judge it by, to hook or anchor it to. If a new experience or idea is different from all past ones, we can very easily reject it for it doesn't fit the paradigm we have created. Doubt, as you will now know, creates the same reaction as belief. Because we have attached to (or judged) every past event, we have automatically imbued them all with an emotion that then colours each new experience.

This "hooking" is very helpful for several reasons:

It gives us a greater feeling of security in our world – otherwise every experience and thought would be "new" (without any previous reference point) and to be able to absorb five hundred new thoughts a minute over a whole life-time would be too much to take – we would all explode in early childhood!

This "hooking" is also very useful for it gives us a remembering that goes to our subconscious and we, therefore, don't have to relearn how to breathe, swallow, walk and so on, each time we want to do those things.

This automatic "hooking" also helps us to jump out of the way of cars, fists, tigers and other dangerous things, quickly and without thinking. It has probably saved your life and/or health many times.

So this "hooking" is not to be sneered at – it is very helpful for survival, but it does have some drawbacks.

Because of our reliance on hooking, having used it for almost every experience to date, we find it very hard to accept new experiences and ideas. If we come across a new idea which does not fit our existing paradigm, we might do one of two things: We either reject the idea (it doesn't really exist) and our selective hearing is very helpful here, or we incorporate the idea into our reality, but with slight variations. So if a new idea comes along, we add to it from our previous experience so it fits our existing paradigm – we actually see something which is different from the "actual" idea. A change in reality occurs and (because hooking is, by now, automatic) we are unaware of the change.

Observe the way new ideas are changed or ignored by your mind-self – it's an interesting exercise!

Nothing is nothing, as well

Nothing is nothing is nothing.

So far, we have always been, so we find it hard to conceive of the experience of not being. The experience of not being, or not experiencing, is not familiar and, therefore, not able to be hooked into. To make this very unfamiliar experience (the one of not being) one that we can allow into our paradigm of past experiences, we give nothingness some substance. This substance we give a name and some of those names are negative, (d)evil, fear and darkness. You will know of many other names you have used or heard of.

For most people, therefore, it is quite difficult to imagine nothing, though you may now be starting to experience it for the first time, from the spaces between thoughts.

The opposite of negative, evil, fear and darkness is positive, g(o)od, love and light. The former are simply not, are nothingness, are lack of the latter.

Imagine, if you will, a house that has been in darkness for one hundred years. You now enter it with a bright torch. The moment you enter, it is filled with light. You turn on the lights and pull open the curtains and the house is immediately bathed in light, for as long as you choose. The darkness is simply the lack of the light. The darkness wasn't even there for it is not anything – it is simply a lack of light.

The darkness does not say, "Hold on, I've been here for a hundred years. Please give me some time to move out". There is no darkness stuck to the walls or etched in the glass. If it had been a something (say, cigarette smoke or dust) it would remain for a time and gradually fade. There is nothing of the nothingness to remain so it is not there – and never was.

You may go into a house that is filled with light, in order to bring some darkness - how do you do that? You cannot. You are bringing in nothing to the something. Only light is there.

When you try to fight with the darkness you always lose, for you are fighting with something that isn't there, so it cannot be reduced or vanquished. You will always lose and so you see the darkness (or evil, negative or fear) as being very powerful. The power you see in it is the power you give it so that you can hook it into past experiences of all things existing. Non-existence is not a viable option.

Fighting includes both the active pushing away of a thing, as well as the passive denial of it. Both are ineffective.

You will always lose if you fight the nothingness (or whatever you call it) for you are always fighting your own altered reality. The only way to move from the nothingness to the somethingness is to bring in the somethingness. No effort, no fighting. Just turn on the light and all is immediately light.

If you try to fight fear you will lose. If you bring in love all you have is the somethingness of love. Fear is only the absence of love.

If you try to fight or deny the demons in your psyche you will always lose. Simply play with the angels in your soul and you fly lightly. The demons were never there – they were never anywhere for they never were. Simply an absence of angels.

If you try to fight anger you will always lose. If you bring in compassion all you will have is compassion. Anger was only the absence of compassion.

If you try to fight loneliness you will always lose. Just bring in companionship and all you have is companionship. Loneliness is a nothingness. It is simply a lack of companionship.

If you try to destroy evil or negative thoughts you will always lose. Simply bring in positive thoughts. Negative thoughts are nothingness – they are simply the absence of positive thoughts.

Don't fight for starting to fight means that you intend to lose. Losing is just an absence of winning. You were born to win, not to fight – be still and allow the winning to happen.

Keep it simple. Keep it lazy. Just hold the torch of your desire and it is there – the nothingness is not.

Activity Versus Action

The difference between activity and action is that activity is what you do, while action results in achievement.

How many things are you doing at this moment? Yes, you're reading a book. Now, what else are you doing? Nothing? You're not even …
Playing with your hair,
Scratching your cheek,
Rubbing your arm,
Tapping your foot,
Swinging your leg,
Biting your lip,
Tapping your fingers,
Smoothing this page,
Nodding your head,
Playing with your jewellery,
Wriggling in your seat,
Stretching your neck,
Grinding your teeth,
Alternately reading and looking around,
Hoping no-one will disturb you right now,
Looking at the beautiful/horrible weather,
Thinking of the nice/horrible weather,
Thinking about dinner,
Thinking of your partner/children,
Looking around at every noise, or
Any other things of no relevance to the reading and understanding

of this book? If you aren't doing at least two of the above, you are truly a remarkable human. The "chatter" that goes on in our mind and with our body is ceaseless and unconscious. We don't even know we are doing it and we're never not doing it. On and on it goes, for no apparent reason, constant chatter and we are not who we are without it.

Then, we are asked to make a speech or give a presentation and so are given some basic lessons. The hardest to learn is to keep our gestures "economic", stand still and not wave our hands around too much. We find it so hard to keep still. Why? Why do we spend so much effort on unproductive activity and then say we don't have time or energy for productive pursuits? Of course, the easy answer is that the things we like are easy to do and our "lack of energy" or "lack of time" excuses really mean, "I don't enjoy that."

The worst punishment for a human is to have a succession of days and nights with absolutely nothing to do. We all know this and that's why prisons were invented. The nothingness is worse than anything else. Why? Perhaps we are afraid of ourselves.

With nothing else to do or think, the only one we can be with is ourselves.

Momentus living

Moment-us = us in the moment

Taking one day at a time is not an easy thing to do, though it's something we're continually encouraged to do. To look at this moment and not the next, or the last, seems to require a great amount of discipline and focus. There's always remembering, reminiscing, dreaming, regretting and thanking. Then there's always planning, deciding, hoping, expecting and dreaming. So much to do in the past and the future but nothing in the middle, for the art of living in the moment is about doing nothing – simply being, simply observing, simply still and simply simple.

We are told to emulate children for that is how they exist, with the implication being that if children can do it then adults must be able to – children are so much less capable than us bigger people. And, as a "big" person, you feel less worthy in some way when you cannot do that thing that seems so natural and easy for lesser mortals. "If they can do it, I must be able to do it", and so you push yourself, criticise and judge yourself and, all the while, it gets harder to do this stillness thing.

Looking not at your soles and where you're going but at your soul and where you are now.

We will look at ways of momentus living soon, but, first, let's see why non-momentus living is not good for your health:

Ex-peccare-tionis

The word *expectation* is derived from the Latin – *Ex* meaning *from the past*, *peccare* meaning *sin* and *tionis* meaning *a condition*. Literally, it means "bringing a sinful condition forward from the past", which is what we do when we hook past events, hold them as truths and "know" similar future events will bring identical feelings or results. This is expectation. We repeat past actions and are not surprised that the same things result. We expect, therefore we get.

To do it differently is to take action with no expectation at all. We simply do. No result is awaited, no feeling is looked for. Simply do. It's really fun to try and not easy for you have had many years of being trained the other way. I urge you to play with it (it is fun!) and you will find that you can experience a previously unpleasant activity, resulting in a pleasant outcome or feeling. It may be:

Eating a food you previously detested,
Inviting a boring/hurtful person around for coffee,
Wearing no shoes in the rain,
Telling someone you like them,
Cleaning your car,
Doing your tax return,
Being alone for four days,
Saying "no" to someone,
Saying "yes" to yourself,
Holidaying in places you didn't like before,
Meditating when you feel like it and then being late for work …

I am sure you can think of a hundred other things as well. A friend of mine calls himself a "constructive destabilisation representative" and this is what you are being to yourself – breaking old patterns in a fun way and for a constructive purpose.

Not only will you have broken a previous pattern (giving you a little more freedom), but you will have transcended your past and, hence, yourself. Start in little ways and, as you gain confidence, launch into bigger and bigger projects to free yourself from your past and from any expectation of particular results. Expectation brings forward "sin" or a lesser result, for that is what we hook into easier. Allowing expectation to take a back seat for a while, with no-one driving but your own automatic pilot, will always give you a better result than before.

How to stop your enlightenment

There is much talk of ascension and enlightenment and the things you need to do to become closer to God, a better person, enlightened, ascended, more in touch with yourself, a happier person or whatever you like to call it. There are many people who will tell you how to ascend or how to alight and many of them will make much money from telling you. Someone else's Ten Steps To Heaven or Twelve Enlightenment Exercises may well be good for you in some way, but remember, always, they are someone else's steps or exercises. Indeed, because they are someone else's, they may actually slow your progress – always check your own inner knowing before embarking on the bus to somewhere, especially when someone else is driving.

The most important thing to remember, though, is that if you don't do the exercises others prescribe, you will still get to where you want to go. The system has been designed in such a way that you cannot avoid "getting to heaven" or "becoming enlightened" or whatever you call it. In Robin Norwood's book *Why Me Why This Why Now*[6], she describes us as being on a railway track – our lives are predestined and the destination is fixed, with us all going "to God" or "being enlightened". We have control over whether we stand still for a while, whether we decide to go backwards for a while or whether we go forward. We have control over the timing of our journey, but not over our destination. Whether we like it or not, we cannot help but go home. The only thing we can do is to construct exercises to delay our arrival. Doing nothing may speed your trip and it's a lot cheaper than delaying your arrival with someone else's course.

Standing still

So, while you are fiddling with everything - your hair, pen, mobile, computer, the planet - consider what thoughts are going through your mind, apart from thinking what an amazing book this is! As you play with your hair, are you thinking of a pleasant past event. And as

---

6   *Why Me Why This Why Now?* by Robin Norwood, Arrow Books, U.K., 1995.

you scratch your chin, are you planning something tomorrow. Each "activity" (which is unnecessary action for this moment) is a clue that you are not in the moment and also a clue as to which other (past or present) moment you are in. Just observe your activity and see where your thoughts lead you. Every moment is a good place to be so enjoy it, wherever it is.

The only thing you could be mindful of, though, is that you can only take action in the present moment and activity occurs in all other moments. Do you want to move forward in this moment or do you want to play in another moment? Play is important and so is action. Just know that you can choose either.

And when you are ready to take that step forward, simply take the Three Steps to Heaven – your steps to heaven, or wherever else you want to go.[7]

---

[7] See the chapter, *Where Did I Leave My Dream?*

Drinking Deep Of Life

We're given two beautiful gifts that we cannot refuse – birth and death. In between these is a space which must be filled with something. What are you doing with your space?

You will know that live spelt backwards is evil. Evil is not bad, it is just the opposite of living. You are given, on this Earth, the opportunity of many experiences and through these, you find yourself and you find that no experience is necessary, that all is inside. But you cannot have that realization until you have ventured, experienced, experimented, lived.

You cannot know what a beautiful place you live in until you have been to other places. Foreigners say much nicer things about our city than do the locals. Friends say much nicer things about me than I can think of. We must travel out to find that the most wondrous journey is in.

The Prodigal Son

You may also know the story of the farmer who had two sons – one stayed on the farm, worked diligently and helped his father and the family a great deal. A good son. The other son went away, had many adventures and squandered the fortune bestowed upon him. On his return, he was lauded as a great and wonderful son.

The good son was sad and angry. He wanted to know of his father why he had never had such a reception when he had done so much for his father – he had been so good. It just wasn't fair!

Existence celebrates your return, not your being there. If you stay on the good road, you will go round few curves, you will feel few bumps, have few breakdowns, never get lost. Your bumps, curves, breakdowns and losses all add beauty and wholeness to your being. You are becoming alive. You are becoming full. You are becoming simple in a simple and beauteous world.

If you stay on the good road, you become the straight line, forever going nowhere. You become a simpleton in a complicated world. You return from nowhere so no celebration is due to you.

If you hide in your sanctuary for fear of doing something wrong, you are simply not living.

Water and cell phones

We see many adults walking around still carrying their dummies. They are old children, fearing to leave their parents. Some of these dummies are in the shape of cell phones and some in the shape of water bottles.

The cell phone carriers think they are telling the world that it cannot do without them, that they are so important and indispensable. What they are actually telling the world is that they are afraid to be alone and they are frightened of not being wanted. So they hold fast and suckle on their little black nipples, hoping their mother will nourish them with acceptance – hiding in their cells and afraid to leave their parents.

The water bottle carriers are afraid of the wholeness of life, the free bounty that's theirs. Perhaps they feel they don't deserve to be so well looked after so they proudly tell the world they are nourishing themselves well.

So many people have it in their mind that they must drink lots of water and, sadly, most of them think this water must be cold. It is like white wine – the experts say it must be drunk cold. Why? They are afraid of the wholeness within.

Firstly, if you know anything of the Ayur Vedic Medicine, you will know that cold liquid is bad for your body in so many ways. Physiologically, the harm is similar to smoking and, like smoking, it becomes habitual – you cannot go anywhere without your bottle.

The second thing is that when you cool a liquid you take away its taste. You have nothing to savour. You are simply taking in a liquid that goes in and out again – a purely mechanical process with no feeling of fulfillment. You are passing strangers in the street and no one is being fulfilled – coming and going and no exchange of energy.

If your liquid is at room temperature its full taste returns, its full presence is there for you. Now, when you drink, you are having a deep and fulfilling conversation with a friend and both your souls are transformed. The water is enlivened. You are enlivened. You are both experiencing something, journeying somewhere. You live. It lives.

It is interesting to note that in the U.S.A., where the idea of iced water predominates, it is very hard to find someone in the street who will return your eye contact and smile. Many are too afraid to drink of the fullness that is life and they hide in the unsafe sanctuary of their cells.

Asking those who don't know

If you want to find something, go and ask the person who has none of it. If you need counselling after a broken marriage, don't go to a happily married person. If you are trying to deal with having been raped, find someone else who has had the same shattering experience; someone else who doesn't yet have their wholeness back. You are searching for something, so ask the one who is also looking. You will discover it together.

If you want to know about water, ask those who have very little of it – the Aborigines. They will tell you that we all drink too much of it. They thrive on much less, for every drop that passes their lips is savoured, appreciated, loved and experienced – the goodness derived is a thousand-fold; maybe a million-fold. It's the quality and not the quantity that gives fulfillment.

If you were to truly savour the beauty of a deliciously strong cup of coffee while in deep, animated and intimate conversation with a close friend, you would be giving yourself more goodness than you would with your cold, sterile and tasteless fifteen gallons of water that you pour through your body each day without a thought.

Why do you think that people say "Grace" before a meal? The thankfulness and appreciation provides more nourishment than does all the vitamins, minerals, carbohydrates and other substances.

Do not be afraid of the water. Taste it. Savour it. Live it. Give yourself to it. It will give back. It will live back. You can then save your arms and put your bottle down, for its contents will move with you and your soul, wherever you are.

Un-possess it.

Love it.

Philip J Bradbury

Leave it.
Live it.

Giving life to life

And so with your life – live deep, live well, live with a flourish, make mistakes with style. Dare yourself to be the tallest poppy in the field, risking the greatest of giving and losing. Wear yourself out, extend yourself and sleep the sleep of exhausted fulfilment. Meditate with fullness, stand in a queue with style, go window-shopping with a vengeance and procrastinate at top speed.

Whatever you do, give it your fullest for the measure of your giving will be the measure of your receiving, will be the speed of your growth, will be the pace of your enlightenment, will be the expansion you bring to the rest of the world.

Action, not activity.

The Energy Of Dreams

Your dreams are a promise from your future – if you deny them, you deny the best that you are capable of.

You already know about the fact that all there ever was, is and will be, is energy. If you have total recall of that knowing, go and have a coffee break, while I remind those who cannot remember[8]. It is helpful to know this so that you can see how to turn your dreams into reality, into solid things you can see, hear, smell, taste and touch.

Science and scientists

If you were to zoom in on an atom (say, hydrogen) you would see a proton surrounded by an electron. If you then zoomed in on that proton you would begin to see, as it grew before your eyes, its substance, its solidity, disappear. There is no core to the proton – it is simply a swirling mass of energy, as is the electron.

If you were to then expand that atom to the size of the Yankee football stadium, you would have, in the middle of the pitch, a pea-sized proton and a smaller object swirling around the perimeter as the electron. The rest is empty space. So that's what you are composed of – 99.9999% empty space, interspersed by minute bundles of swirling energy. And so it is with rocks, trees, caterpillars, hamburgers and toilet-rolls.

Although the Newtonian scientific model (of the billiard balls and all things being separate physical elements) has been superseded by the Einsteinian model (of all things being composed of energy) 99.9999%

---

[8]   See the chapter, *Your Always Knowing*, about your remembering.

of scientists still operate in the Newtonian sphere of thought. Because Einstein's ideas cannot be attached or hooked to any previous experience, they are not absorbed by the scientific community. The words of Einstein have been read, studied, talked about and agreed with – but not digested.

Scientists remain in the Newtonian paradigm[9] even while they know it is outdated and incorrect. The courage to move on is not there and they exhibit a very understandable human irrationality. However, the great sadness is that until they can move into a paradigm of reality, the stuff taught to our children (and to you) will remain outdated, inappropriate and illogical. People look to science to explain life and even when scientists lose the plot and have no explanations, humans retain their "hook", which is that scientists know. To let that hook go is to have to say to yourself "I know". While that is true, your training to date may have been to look to others for your answers.

In summary, then, the reason we have not totally embraced the reality of our energetic selves is, in general, people are hooked into the wisdom of those who are hooked into an obvious lie. And while the idea of the energy essence of things will be easy to accept in your heart (your knowing space) it may not be so easy for your head or understanding space.

If you feel the need to understand something you will find yourself asking the wrong questions; questions in the belief/doubt mode, like:

"Does it agree with me?"

"Do you agree with me?"

Will it make me admit error?"

"Will it make me look silly?"

"Do I fear this change?"

"Can I make this change of belief?"

And other questions that have no relationship to the actual problem.

The head needs to understand, to remember, to dismember. It needs each little piece of the puzzle to fit into the existing paradigm. Any individual part of the whole that doesn't fit is thrown away. It needs to have a logical sequence and hook for each dismembered part, so that it can be justified and explained to the self and the outer world. The whole is irrelevant, the parts are important and what the outer world thinks is paramount.

[9] A paradigm is a pattern we create, a preconceived way we choose to see our world.

The heart, however, has no need of understanding. It simply perceives the whole, asks no questions and immediately feels the truth or otherwise, without needing to know why it's right – or to explain why it's right. No explanation, no justification, no proof, no examination, no dismembering – simply a feeling and a knowing about the wholeness. There is no acceptance or rejection for nothing is owned – there is simply a knowing and an allowing for things to be. Nothing has to "fit" or not fit – all can just be, unpossessed, and can be taken from or added to at any time.

So do not be surprised if this "energetic" idea is new or hard to grasp, for the so-called experts have not been able or willing to, yet. Your head may have trouble but your heart won't. Read the words and put them in your heart – if they feel good in there, simply allow them to be. If they don't, allow them, also, to be.

Energetic body language

The idea goes like this:
Everything is made of energy, vibrating at different rates. The slower it vibrates the more solid it is. So, air vibrates faster than your tears which vibrate faster than your eye-lid which vibrates faster than your crockery. Those are things you can see and touch. The same goes for other things which we sense in different ways – scents move or vibrate slower than sounds which move slower than light which moves slower than thought.

The speed of light is said to be about 328,000 miles per second while sound goes at about 176,000 miles per second. Two important things to remember here:

1. These speeds are dependant on gravity (i.e. planet size) and are different on different sized planets, and

2. There are not distinct "steps" of speed for each type of energy - it is a continuum. Ultra-violet light moves faster than yellow which moves faster than infra-red and, within that, the different yellows move at different speeds.

A stone is simply a thought slowed down. A rainbow is a tree sped up, a tree is a rock sped up. All are made of the same substance and the only difference between you and your car is the speed at which you vibrate.

Now, look at your body as you stand – at the top is your brain which detects thought. Next down are your eyes which "see" light, ears for sound, nose for smell, tongue for taste and hands at the bottom for touch. We are built as the universe (the image of God?) – the higher the body-part, the higher are the vibrations it resonates and connects to.

Some might argue that taller people must, therefore, be more intelligent but as I'm not an extremely tall fellow, I cannot allow that into my present paradigm!

Dreaming your reality

So how to manifest your dreams? By now, some of you may feel the knowing of it creeping up on you, returning to your memory-places.

A dream is simply the vibration of all that is, at the speed of thought. The dream of a tree is, in fact, that tree sped up to the speed of light or thought. The dream of a holiday is all the elements of that holiday, all sped up to the speed of thought. So that's why you can move about with lightning (or faster) speed in your dream reality but not in your awake reality. Different realities vibrate at different speeds.

So, if you can speed these realities up every night, in your dreams, why can't you slow them back down? Well, the fact is that you do, every living moment.

You hear many people continually say, "There's never enough time – I'm always late." And they are! Their attitude to time creates their lateness and their verbalising it ensures that it continues. Your energy of attitude is slowed down to the vibration of actuality.

How many amazingly optimistic people do you know who just seem to be lucky? Their attitude vibration is transmuted into the vibration of actual luck – they know they are lucky so they are.

You know of your future by what you are thinking now – as you think, so you say and, therefore, you receive:

Imagination ➔ expression ➔ action

What sort of future do you want to create for yourself? Think on it, imagine it, hold the dream and watch it emerge.

Your Always Knowing

We're constantly taught to think, learn and remember – beyond those is the profound simplicity of knowing.

The word *education* comes from the Latin, *educere*, which means to draw forth something that is already there. All you will ever need to learn is presently within and there is nothing you don't know. There is nothing you have to learn. This is the difference between a teacher and a master.

Teachers and Masters

A teacher will tell you that you need to listen, to remember, to practise, to look up to them, for they have (in their possession) something they can give you. They see their knowledge as a thing, a thing to be sold and/or passed on to others who want, and do not have, that thing. This puts them, as you might imagine, in a higher place than you – a place you look up to – and, in some way, they have some control over you. They can, if they choose, decide to give you only certain parts of the thing they have and they can hold on to other parts. This way, they can keep you attached to them, always wanting more and seeing them as better in some way. Also, because you don't know what you don't know, they can pretend that there is always more you need to learn from them and keep you on a string. If you choose to be with a teacher, there is no wrong. However, just be aware that when someone allows you to feel that their knowledge and skills are greater than yours, it is often because their need of having (and not actual having) is greater than yours. If you look up to them, their esteem tanks fill very quickly. If you fill someone else's tank, make sure that it's not at the expense of yours.

A master is different. A master knows nothing. A master does not tell you what you need to know, where you need to look, how you need to look. A master allows you to decide what you need to learn and stands beside you (not above you) to help you find your own way to your own remembering. A master simply reflects back to you what you already are and already know, so is no higher or lower than you. Sometimes they can see a key you cannot, but they insist you turn it and walk through the door.

Masters do not teach, they remind.

Where did your knowing go?

When you arrived in this world, you brought the full knowing of "Life, the Universe and Everything" with you. You have been here many, many times – hundreds and perhaps thousands of times. Each time you came, you spent a life-time learning things, through teachers, masters and your own experience. Not one scrap of learning has been lost and you have it all with you - every second of every life-time – and you will never lose it. Therefore, you brought in this immense knowledge from all walks of life, all occupations, all ages, all cultures, all attitudes, all locations, all of the all.

You brought the vastness of this in with your tiny body – and all your parents wanted was a nice little boy or girl! What a shock they got! Instead of a cute baby that they could teach everything to, they received a huge bundle that knew it all! They may not have recognised the immense luggage you brought with you, on a conscious level, but they sensed something unexpected arriving. You may have sensed that when your own babies arrived.

If they weren't aware of your great knowing (as most parents aren't) they then set about teaching you the things they thought were important for you. These may not have been the things you thought were important, but you were taught them anyway. Then, when the authorities deemed that you be taught things your parents didn't know (without asking whether your parents did know or not) you were sent to a school – again, to be taught things you already knew, but may not have known that you knew. You needed reminding but not teaching.

Ask yourself - how many times have I been taught something and got the feeling I already knew? Or, it just seemed so simple, or easy.

Or, you just knew what the "teacher" was going to say next. It happens all the time and you are probably only aware of a few of those times.

Sometimes you knew things your parents didn't (or thought they didn't) and you tried to tell them. What was their reaction?

Disbelief?

Ignoring you?

Belittling you?

"How would you know that?"

"You're just making things up!"

"We'll check that with your teacher."

"What does the dictionary say?"

"What does the encyclopaedia say?"

So unbeknown to them, your "big people" systematically and repeatedly told you that you didn't know, and smeared your pure knowing with a thick and sticky layer of doubt in yourself. That doubt eventually masked any knowing you may have felt you had, and so the only way you could learn or know something was to go to an "expert" who did know – that "expert" was never you.

So, your knowing went nowhere, it just got hidden by self-doubt.

You may now ask, "How do I remove that thick and sticky layer of self-doubt to find my all-knowing nature within," and I will say, "Don't remove anything!"

From what you have read, the nothingness of your self-doubt is simply an absence of your knowingness, so rather than try to remove a nothingness (which we cannot), let's bring in a something. How? By retuning your antennae.

The School of Life

Our school motto was *Nil mortalibus ardui est* – nothing is impossible for mortal man. At the time I never thought about it – it was just another bit of grandstanding to give the myth of education more mana than it deserved. Perhaps the "hit and myth" of education would be more apt. However, since leaving that hallowed establishment I have come to realize that education is no hit and miss affair – we learn exactly what we want to learn in the school of life, and we remember exactly what we want to. It therefore follows that we can do anything we want to, for the knowledge to do it is there for the asking.

You probably spent ten to twelve years at school. During that time you were bombarded with an incredible amount of information about the sex life of the worm, the population of Japan, the kings of England, the refractive properties of light, French phrases, soldering metal, making scones, playing tennis and a million and one other things. How much of it did you remember? How much of it did your friends (who were in the same stream of information) remember? You may remember the poem Ozymandius and the works of Byron. Your chemist friend remembers about the covalency of carbon and the Krebs cycle while your accountant friend still recalls learning about compound interest and depreciation. All of that information was there for all of you, but because your antennae were tuned differently, you each received slightly different signals.

There are some people you meet whose antennae are tuned to just about everything. The Mr. Interestings are able to converse with anyone on almost any subject. They are not experts in everything but have a reasonable degree of knowledge and interest in most things. The intriguing thing about these people is that they are not only interesting – they are also interested. They are not boastful – they are simply interesting people who like to learn about everything and like to pass on that knowledge to anyone else who wants to learn. They not only want to tell you fascinating things, but they want to hear fascinating things from you – and that is the secret of their knowledge. They have a thirst or a yearning for it and it comes to them.

Compare Mr. Interesting with Mr. Dullard who is deeply into his pet (and only) subject – say golf. Once he has finished his discourse on how he eagled the 9th, parred the 14th and drowned in the 19th, you want to tell him how you climbed Everest, walking on your hands while eating spaghetti with your feet, in only three hours. What happens? His eyes glaze over and you can see his mind going back to that second hole where he sliced the ball. The one-sided conversation dies for lack of interest. He knows about golf and nothing else. He does not want to know about anything else. He is perplexed, however, that other people know so much about other things.

The Master of your Life

Some people have an interesting view of God. Instead of hir being a separate entity somewhere, judging and marking the score-card of our lives, that entity is everywhere and is everything. We are all a part of God and therefore know everything that God knows. We are, they say, radio receiver antennae, standing in the flow of all radio frequencies – the flow of all knowledge. To recognize any particular part of that knowledge (or particular frequency) all we have to do is tune our antennae to the correct frequency. So how do we tune our antennae? All we have to do is simply open our minds and say "I want to know about that subject". If we sincerely want to know, our brain, through our pituitary and pineal glands, will receive that knowledge. The only limit to our knowledge is the limit we put on our willingness to explore.

Whether you believe in that concept of God or not does not matter. It is, however, an interesting way to look at yourself and your life. You are the God or Master of it. You control your feelings, beliefs, finances, future, dreams, relationships, body and even the lessons and people who come into your life. You, within yourself, also know everything there is to know about your life and all life in general. You know how to succeed (even in hard times) and you know how to fail. You have more knowing and more choices than you are aware of.

So how do you get access to and use the amazing power and knowledge that is there for the taking?

I have a friend, a builder, who is quite open about the fact that he flunked everything at school – English, Maths, Science, Geography, everything. One day I saw him drawing up plans for a house to be built on a very steep slope. He was calculating the angles for trusses, the weight and size of beams, the depth and width of the substantial foundations and all of this required advanced mathematics and geometry.

I said to him, "David, I thought you said that you were useless at mathematics. This maths you are doing here is pretty complicated."

"Oh no it's not", he said, "This isn't maths, it's building."

All of those complicated mathematical calculations which were so difficult at school, were now second nature, now that they related to his main interest in life. Now that they had a different label (building, not maths) and he now really wanted to know, the information had become available to him.

You are all you need to be

You are an incredibly clever and resourceful being. There is nothing you cannot do. Most of us have two legs, two arms, a stomach, a chest, a head, two eyes, two ears and the other human components.

If one human can climb Everest, or swim the Channel, or be a chess grand-master, or become a millionaire, then all humans can. Each of those achievements were attained using the same components you have – a very nearly identical body and mind. If a clone of yours can paint beautiful pictures, design computers or perform ballet then so can you. But, as you know, there are prerequisites to achievement:

A ballet dancer does not start dancing at birth – he wants to do it, he practises and then he can do it. Physical abilities require first a desire and then some practise.

Mental abilities are exactly the same. A great scientist will be fascinated by her field of study (a desire) and will read about it, perform experiments and study it more deeply – practise.

The same again goes for business acumen. In the U.S.A. the average millionaire has been bankrupt two and a half times. They have a desire to succeed financially and so they launch their business – learning by their mistakes and advancing by their correct decisions.

So where did all of the successful people find out how to succeed? How did you learn to walk? Did your parents pick up each of your feet and place them down, or did you work it out for yourself, by simply doing it and practising? Just as you knew how to walk from birth, you also knew how to paint pictures, build houses, drive a car and to make money, from birth.

Everything you will ever want to know, is known to you right now. So why aren't you incredibly rich and famous right now? The knowledge you need is within you and around you, but you do not know how to access it. You are standing in the library of the books of life but you have only been interested in reading a few of them. Some you wanted to read but you couldn't reach. Did you ever think of asking the librarian for a ladder? – too much effort or were you too embarrassed to do so?

Your parents, your teachers and your employers have all conspired to instil in you that the only valid knowledge you have is that which they have given you. This conspiracy is not out of malice, but out of ignorance – they had the same "training" as you. You, however, have come to realize a greater awareness and knowledge than just that "given" information. You do not need me to tell you that. You would, though, like some confirmation of your greater awareness and also some guidance towards expanding and using it – this may be why you have led yourself to this book.

Minds are like parachutes – they only work when they are open.

"Life the Universe and Everything" is incredibly complicated and hard to understand – if you want it to be. There will be many out there who will tell you that mastery of life will only come about through paying them or others large amounts of money, in return for advice or training. This sort of helpful advice comes from those who want your money or from those who thrive on drama.

Unfortunately for the dramatists, life is actually very simple and the simpler you make it, the more successful and more fun it will be.

If you come across an expert who cannot explain things in your terms, then (s)he is not an expert. Anyone with a full and profound understanding of their craft can pass that understanding on to the simplest of people. The pretender will cover up hir lack of understanding with a pile of baffling bull-dust.

So be open to parting with some cash, for advice or training, and judge the rightness of it by its simplicity and your being able to easily comprehend it. This includes this book – does it measure up? Please let me know, either way.

Karma (Unedited Version)

The universe exacts no retribution – it simply asks for awareness.

It is interesting that the "New Age" movement is supposed to be about self-responsibility (self-knowing, self-remembering) and yet so many give over their responsibility to others. No difference from non-New Agers. We all do it, irrespective of beliefs.

Many things are taken as unquestioned truths, simply because they have wide acceptance. Because one thought has been hooked in, all other contradictory ones are subsequently missed, as if they never existed.

As was explained to me recently, our brain is like a car park full of cars. Until we drive the old heaps out, the flash new ones can't come in. The older they are, the harder it is to start them and move them out.

Karma explained

Karma is a Sanskrit word and is explained by the Law of Cause and Effect. Under this "Universal" law everything you ever do, or have done, has a consequence. For example, if you cheat someone, you will be cheated on – the universe exacts its own retribution. If you have been a "good" person, you will have good done to you.

For those who believe in the currently popular version of reincarnation, you are what you are now from this "deservability" system. If you were a murderer in a past life, you will probably be murdered in a future one. If you ate beef in a past life, you may very well be killed by a bull in this one. You "earn" Karma by doing naughty deeds or thinking naughty thoughts.

By the same token, you "earn" Dharma by doing good deeds. If you were a saintly person at some previous time, you may have an easy ride this time round. Dharma is also your life purpose and if you find it, you are blessed – it's like a reward for waking up.

Logically and morally, this current idea sounds very equitable – the universe always keeps the scales of justice balanced. The other good thing with this system is that it doesn't matter whether or not you get caught doing good or bad deeds by humans – the Universe (you may call it God) knows all, and rewards or punishes in a perfectly equitable way. There is no way out of the system and all debts and bonuses are called up at some time. No one is exempt.

One problem with this system is that we can never get out of it as we are in a constant state of interaction with our fellow beings, with other creatures, plants and the Earth. As it is impossible to be "perfect" human, bull, grasshopper or whatever, every living second of our lives and it is impossible to be perfect, all the time, to all other things, we're always in debt to the system. The result is that there will always be something to "sort out" and it's a never-ending treadmill which we never get off.

"So," you may ask, with justification, "how do I ever advance if I am forever paying debts from my last twenty lifetimes, including this one?" The answer is that under this system, it is practically impossible. That's one of the disadvantages of the system.

One of the advantages (apart from its theoretical equity) is that it saves having to make hard decisions. Several people in unsatisfactory relationships have said that they are still in the relationship because of a past debt they owe to their partner. I know it's not easy having to leave any relationship, but handing over your power to a karmic debt system does nothing for your feeling of self-empowerment and, hence, your ability to exercise that power. Far better to admit that it's hard to let go and then you are claiming the reality (and the resulting power) as yours.

You have more power and ability to change things if you admit you can't handle them than if you pretend you can when you can't. Admitting helplessness opens the way for others to come in and help.

The original idea of Karma was reconstituted by religious leaders to ensure their flock remained "good" – i.e. obeyed their laws. A brilliant control mechanism! So, for that and other reasons, this human law has assumed cosmic or universal law status because the many have not questioned the few and because it is so very convenient, at times.

That's a brief explanation of the currently popular version of karma – we'll now look at the original version.

You have nothing to learn

The in-vogue version of karma is that you are here to right past wrongs but, in truth, you are not here to learn anything. Part of the "adjusted" Karmic Law is that, through lessons learned and debts repaid, you improve and advance. Sorry, not true.

This misconception has come about through the observation of peoples' behaviour. It may have become apparent to you that people tend to learn things quickest when they make mistakes, and sayings abound to keep us in that belief:
- No gain without pain,
- The finest metal comes from the hottest fire,
- It's the rough that gives us the grip and the smooth that we slip over on,
- Pruning makes the roses grow stronger,
- I learned more from getting up than from falling down,
- Every cloud has a silver lining, and on and on they go, giving us comfort when we fall or lose something – the pain and/or loss is our greatest learning.

This is so for those who believe in it but it doesn't have to be that way. It is possible to learn from our triumphs but, because of our mind-hook system, our losses and pains are the experiences most choose to learn from.

Karma restated

The original Karmic Law was tampered with by a group of frightened clergy who saw their "flock" realizing a greater truth than what they were preaching. They thought that the only way they could hold sway over their flock (subjects?) was to impose their rule of fear.

The original (untampered) Karmic Law was that of Finding Yourself by Finding Your Not-self – to realize Who You Really Are by simply realizing who you aren't. This is also called the rule of Cause and Effect and simply means that when you do something against your nature, you will know about it. You are not punished by God – you are simply given the realization that it wasn't right for you. Each time you become *Who You Really Aren't*, you know about more of *Who You Really Are*.

A friend had a drinking problem and was often told not to drive while drunk, by well-meaning friends. He was gently warned. He ignored these warnings and had an accident – no real injuries to himself and minor damage to the car. He ignored that slightly louder warning and then had a bigger smash, involving the police (who suspended him from driving for a month) and a broken arm. Larger warning. Still not listening. The last accident saw him in hospital for a month, with permanent facial scarring, major back injury, written-off car and loss of licence for three years. He now drinks no alcohol.

So the idea is simply to listen and be able to say, "O.K., I've got the message. I'm sorry and I won't do that again." Accept, forgive, change.

You may wonder why some people are born with terrible defects or disadvantages – surely those are karmic debts! The original Karmic Law would say explain it this way: We are all here to find out Who We Really Are and we'll all learn that in different ways. For some people, their decision is to learn that through being crippled or "disadvantaged" in some other way. Being crippled is not a punishment but simply the best perspective, for some people, for seeing Who They Really Are. In fact, being crippled (mentally or physically) could mean a very happy and contented life – many of these people never need to work and struggle to sustain themselves and they are cosseted from birth to death. Their lives are different from ours but different does not necessarily mean worse. The other consideration is that those whose lives are touched by a "cripple" learn much about themselves (Who They Really Are) from their having to care for such a person. The idea of punishment and reward is a human perception one and not a cosmic one.

The committing of a crime does not mean that you need to have that crime committed against you – if you accept your wrongdoing and change your behaviour, you've paid your karmic debt – you've learned what's right for you.

Bill Cosby, American comedian, publicly admitted that, as a younger man, he was unfaithful to his wife many times. After a time, however, he came to realize what was important in his life and two of those were:

- His feelings about himself, and
- His wife.

He recognized his error, forgave himself and righted the wrong (for him) and now spreads the message of "good" family values to millions of people through his television programs.

Under the adapted system he would have had to (in this life or another) endure an unfaithful partner. Under the original karmic system, he has now "paid" his karmic debt and is realizing and living a greater truth for himself and inspiring others to consider that same truth.

Experience → Learning → Expansion

Learning the easy way

Life was not meant to be a struggle but we have been "trained" from birth that it is and, like Karma, wide acceptance has created a universal law.

The only thing you have come here for is to remember who you are and if you choose to remember by falling off, then go for it. If you choose to remember by staying on and having a beautiful ride, then that's your best way. The choice is yours and don't forget to exercise that choice!

The Circle Of Life, The Wheel Of Change

Like the snake and the crab, we are constantly growing and must regularly shed our "skin" – resistance to that shedding causes us what we call "pain".

The only constant is change and all change is a constant. Look not to what you are losing and gaining within a change process (for that is often a mere distraction) but look to the core of the change – within that core you will see a connection to every other change in your life. Whether you are looking at a change in politics, relationships, health, work or a way of thinking or relating, you will see a similarity to all other changes. And that similarity? The becoming of *Who You Really Are*.

As you pass through the doorway of a change, listen to your soul, the usher at that doorway. What is being asked of you? What is it you are to be looking at? What is it that you are to be acknowledging? If you can still yourself for a moment during a period of change (not always easily done) and listen to the whispers through your being, you may discern two messages:

The first message may be about your graduation ceremony. You would not be allowed through the door if you had not earned the right and you are being asked to look to your talents, your beauty and your power. You are being asked to look at what you have learned and become. You will not pass easily through that door unless you are able to celebrate your achievements and the beauty that now shines from your soul. So gather those talents to your heart and acknowledge the great steps you have taken and reward yourself appropriately. You are not a refugee of your old state, you are a graduate.

The second message will undoubtedly be of the next course you are to undertake. It will tell of the new subjects you are to learn and may even tell a little of the teachers you are to apprentice to. With a map of your next journey, you will make it more quickly and joyfully and, who knows, without getting lost or sidetracked along the way.

So, look not to the outer dramas but listen to the inner whispers and we all wish you well on your next little trip – may it be filled with more joy and peace than the last one.

Birth, death and all that

The only constant in your life, as you know, is change – have I already said that? I don't change much do I!

Change, inevitable change. Change abhorred. Change welcomed. Change regretted. Change celebrated.

Whatever the nature of your changes (or your reaction to them) they will persist, either violently throwing you or gently placing you in a new place that can seem bewildering, exciting, scary, amusing, disorienting, refreshing or all of these together. And the change will continue long after you've gone – it's more permanent than your body, your car, your house, your friendships, your shoreline and your forests. Denial of or resistance to change is a denial of your strongest reality, your grandest truth and, hence, of the core of your being and the greatness of your potential.

We cannot halt the changes within our bodies – the growth from childhood to adulthood, the subtle changes that tell of our move to wisdom years and the eventual gifting back to the earth from where we came, as we successfully complete another cycle of change.

And while each new cycle of change is very different, they all have an amazing similarity to each other. Whether it's your birth, your first day at school, your first period, your first erection, your first love, marriage, divorce, new job, redundancy, serious illness, first child, first grandchild or last breath, all are a death. All are a shedding of the old and growth of the new. All have the potential for pain and pleasure and with every one we grow a little wiser, a little more serene and a little more honest, for there is nothing so conducive to a bout of honesty as a death. With each death and rebirth, big or small, we are, again, confronted with one or more of our frailties and, yet again, we are asked to acknowledge one or more of our strengths. Whether or not we confront or acknowledge (or even observe) ourselves as we pass from one room to another, through the doorway of change, is up to us. If we do, however, we learn a little more of who we are and, hence, fulfil our only purpose for being here – that of realising the fullness of who we are.

If we can honestly confront and acknowledge ourselves at these times of change, we find that we can move through each succeeding change with greater ease, grace and serenity. Soon we hardly notice the changes as we open ourselves to our own honesty.

Creating ripples

You well know that the moment you make a decision to change or move, your world is forever different. You cannot move a finger without moving the air. You cannot make a decision without it rippling to another. Even if no action is taken, the thought of action flows to those who will be affected. Whether you are aware of it or not, their inner senses detect a change in your inner senses.

If you are a (say) married woman, wanting a little more freedom to do the things important to you, you may notice your husband becoming more possessive or suspicious, even before you have said or done anything. It's as if his inner senses cause his body to react even while he's unaware of his change in behaviour.

So look not to others for the reason, but to your own movements in desire and perception, and you will see the power you have within to affect change on this planet. You may not even be aware of the minute changes within, but they will surely be reflected in how others relate to you.

- Are people becoming more friendly? – are you liking yourself more?
- Are people criticising you more? – are you being more self-critical?
- Are people being more giving to you? – are you giving more to yourself?
- Are you being denied opportunities? – are you feeling less deserving of life's opportunities?
- Are people listening to you more? – are you listening to your own inner voice more?
- Are people opening more doors for you? – are you now prepared to move forward?

You cannot have a thought or action without some reaction on another part of the planet. As you toss your stone of resolution into the yielding pond of universal acceptance, the ripples will surely travel the full distance of that universe. No stone is rejected or thrown back and all are allowed their unique ripples.

On their way to the edge, your ripples will meet many other ripples – some will flow with and speed yours along while others will cross and disturb yours. On the way, too, your ripples may encounter other objects in the pond. There may be a rock or two which bounces your ripples back to you and disturbs your pattern – people who have no desire for change and will resist your need for change. The disturbance caused here is not "the evil you do to them" but the fear they see for themselves as a consequence of your change – "the evil they do to themselves". Know, too, that the pond is not filled with these rocks, though the disturbed ripples will seem more noticeable than the smooth ones. There are many more calm ones if you choose to focus on them. And these smoother ripples, ever expanding, may pick up and push along those floating on the surface. You cannot help but help others along if they, too, wish to move with the flow. It is not your intention to move anyone but yourself but you will, nevertheless, help someone else, though you may be unaware of the effect and force of your ripples.

Without judgement or reaction, simply become the Silent Witness to the ripples you observe.

The constant pattern of change

If you were to look back on the multitude of different changes you've been through, you may be able to discern a pattern, for while the only constant is change, all change is a constant – a repetition of a pattern which, if you look past the outer trimmings to the core, you will see a core that resembles all other cores.

To talk of this core I must first take you back a step to see the core of yourself and you can do this by imagining yourself as being born as a small dry flannel (ready to soak up and absorb all it touches) and growing into a large beach towel, soaked in the wisdom of your experience. As you go through each change you are wrung out, with many old truths being squeezed from your being. You always stay damp, holding to some old truths but you come through a change process feeling wrung out, having lost something of yourself. The loss is not, however, of yourself, but of a truth that no longer serves you well.

These truths can be patterns of seeing yourself, of seeing your world, of belief, of behaviour, of acting, of relating or of interests. Or they can be possessions, jobs or friends that don't comfortably fit the shape of your new reality. You are capable of massive change and if you look back on the things or people you were interested in, the way you related to people, or the beliefs you had, you may be amazed at how many once-upon-a-time truths have been wrung from your soul. And with each wringing-out you have become a little more aware, serene and whole. Through change you give away to receive more of yourself.

After each change you are a little drier, larger and more able to absorb new truths.

Those of you whose grace has allowed the changes to move through you with such ease that there is no stillness between the changes, no breathing spaces, no stopping and starting in your life, are truly blessed. Your being is one of unrelenting and continual change. The change has become so constant and fluid that there appears no change at all and you are able to move beyond the changes and simply be. You are the stillness born of the no-stillness and are all the power and beauty you are capable of – a rock unmoved by the changes around you and a hollow reed bending in the wind, allowing the changes to whisper through your soul. Bending and unbending. Moving and unmoving. You are not changed but you have become the process, the change, and with simplicity you inspire us and stand above the crowd with grace, stillness and wisdom.

If you are still struggling with change and are finding it a bumpy and uncomfortable ride, it may help to imagine yourself, before a change, in a pleasant room in which all your needs are met – a comfortable and familiar place in which to relax. Imperceptibly, though, you begin to grow with no conscious effort on your part. Then suddenly, one day, you realize that you have grown to the size of the doorway and, with a horrifying thought, you know you must now squeeze through that doorway and move to a larger room or even to the limitlessness of the open fields. This is not a comfortable realization but you have more self respect than to stand still and allow yourself to be stifled.

You have no more problems or pain than anyone else. You simply have the courage to say you have them and you must make a move to resolve them. To move, however, you must squeeze yourself through the doorway of change and you have grown to such a size that it will require very determined and well calculated moves to get each part of your swelling body through that constricting hole. So, one body part at a time must go through and sometimes you get the procedure wrong and have to go back and try again a different way. You may start many times, give up, start again and wonder if it's all worth it.

Then you ask if you're worth it, smile a huge smile and know you're worth every grunt, groan, pain and rip as you squeeze through into a larger, more accommodating space.

Practising Your Constant Changes

While your moccasins will walk a different road, the strange fact is that we'll both come across very similar sign-posts.

The "failures" are some of the bravest people I've met – they've had the courage to walk through the doorway of change and experience the expansion they deserve. As we are all unique, there is no one way to do this growth stuff. You've just got to give it a go, for giving it a go is growth in itself.

There is, however, a pattern that may be helpful to bear in mind:

Head first

The first part to go through the doorway of change is your head. You may be in panic mode or feeling very vulnerable or powerless in some way and few of your faculties are working properly. Your heart (memory of past and future) is unsure, your stomach (who you really are) is swirling in confusion and you're feeling too physically weakened to see very far ahead. While your mind is not totally clear you can, with effort, summon up enough inner strength to logically and systematically calculate the next minute's or day's moves to make. Your head is sort-of working while your other faculties are in near shut-down phase. So your head goes through first. You follow your head. You know what is right by the logic of your reasoning.

Think first, feel later.

The tummy tuck

The next part is your stomach, which holds all your strong feelings and related disguises – especially those relating to Who You Really

Are.

At birth you carried a dream, a reason for being here[10] and that may be called your original dream, soul purpose, inner child, identity, self-perception and many other things. We will call it *Who You Really Are* and, at birth, it was centred in your solar plexus or stomach area.

As the lances (expectations, criticisms and manipulations) of others pierced your side, you needed to find ways to protect yourself from these wounds. This Who You Really Are found (very quickly) that the best protection was a series of disguises (for many were needed) that made you look the way others wanted you to – or how you thought others thought you ought to look. And each new mask was a covering for a pain felt from others.

The masks increased as the pains did and, soon, that little bundle of Who You Really Are was encased in a huge array of masks, which did two things:
1. They covered the pain so you couldn't see it, and
2. They gave the world the view of yourself you thought it wanted to see.

Now, for your stomach to fit through this narrow doorway of change, some masks and pains have to be released for you won't fit through if you hold on to them.

This second stage, then, sees you releasing some strong emotions – often ones that have been bottled up and hidden from all (even yourself) for a long time. The change process may see you releasing some feelings of anger, sadness, abandonment, loneliness and a whole range of other "negative" ones. It may feel like you're "losing it" and you are – you're losing the masks of pretence and getting closer to Who You Really Are. It can be a painful time, a confusing time, but one made easier by two things:
1. The knowing that the losing of *Who You Really Aren't* means a gaining of *Who You Really Are*, and
2. Becoming the Silent Witness to your own change process, to your own death and rebirth.

As a pain arises, you simply allow it to happen – the tears, throat-lumps, feelings, bodily pain, emotional turmoil, mental stress – and you observe it happening. The pain may not be any less this way but it moves through quicker and the cleansing and clarity is greater.

---

10 See the chapter, *Where Did I Leave My Dream*

If you worry about the pain or try to analyse it, you slow it down and it possesses you for longer. The more you analyse ("Am I going mad?", "What does this anger mean?", "Where does this sadness come from?") the less you will understand it. Instead, try analysing with your heart by simply allowing the tears, anger, shivers, hot and cold, fears and all the other feelings and manifestations of your disguise-releasing exercise. Allow them to flow away from you, knowing nothing except that you are moving closer to Who You Really Are.

Obviously, you need to find a safe place and time to allow these feelings out, but if you are prepared to fully allow their expression, you will be surprised at how accommodating they are of you, only arriving when you are safe in terms of time, place and supportive friends.

Probably, you will not release all your feelings at one time. However, once you have acknowledged, expressed, accepted and allowed enough of them to go for this transition stage, you will be ready to move to the next phase:

Heart space

You have thought through and felt through your present change process, and it's now time for your heart to move through the doorway of change. As you read previously[11], your true memory is in your heart and, within that, is the knowing of all that is. Your heart also holds the knowing of all that has ever been and all that will ever be. Your heart-knowing was previously covered by all the masks and, now that some have been discarded, you can see a little more of Who You Really Are and what you're really here for. This may take some time. Allow the time.

You may have been going in a particular direction for a long time, thinking you were on the right course. But now, with a little more unfolding of the map, a little more revealing of your true self, you may see that your direction may need to be changed. This can be disconcerting, to say the least. You may have set out to be a doctor and after many years of study and work, you realize your real interest lies in photography. What a waste you may say. You may say many other things as well! But the thing you cannot say is "I'm going back to be a doctor". You may try many times but, somehow, it just doesn't work. And each time you try, the message of Get back to where you once belonged (to

---

11   See the chapter, *Unhooking Your Memory*

quote the Beatles) will be stronger and more painful.

You may ignore the heart-messages and leave this Earth plane unfulfilled in your true passion, or you may listen. Listening is harder and it's easier. Listening means being still and that's very hard. Knowing what your heart is saying is very easy (when you have stopped to listen) for what you are listening to is yourself. The messages you hear may sound a little strange but incredibly right. What you are being asked to do may be something you have never trained or studied for (this time round) but if you give it a go, it will seem so easy and right – as if you have been training for it for lifetimes, which you probably have.

This knowing something you never knew you knew may be a little disconcerting but that's what happens when you listen to your heart. And listen you must for there your purpose, your passion and your fulfilment are. Sometimes, it is only after the rough ride of a change, when you need a rest, that you actually hear those whispers.

A change in one thing will create a need for change in many other things – the ripples go on and on and you never know where they stop. A change in career may trigger a change in friends, which may trigger a change in beliefs, which may trigger a change in partner, and on and on. You think you've just been through a massive change but you do not know that more is to come, unless you stop and listen.

You may consciously create your own stillness at this stage or, more likely, you may be stilled by other forces. Even if your heart wants you to listen and you feel the demand for stillness within, you may ignore it. You have a choice. If you choose not to listen you may find yourself grounded by forces beyond yourself. If it's really important for you to listen, your heart will find a way to still you – it's very resourceful!

Through the second (tummy tuck) phase of change you probably felt the need for many resources – especially friends, therapists and anyone else to lean on, explain and listen to you. In this (heart) phase, though, you may feel the opposite – all you want is your own self and complete silence from the world.

When you enter this stillness phase, many uncomfortable things may happen:
- You may feel guilty, not doing anything,
- You may feel that nothing is happening and it should be,
- You may feel "apart" from the world, unconnected,
- You may question your sanity,

- You may question your role in the world,
- You may start to see serious things as funny,
- You may start to see funny things as serious,
- You may worry about some of your bodily functions and find your body talking to you,
- You may find important things becoming irrelevant,
- You may start thinking seriously about irrelevant things,
- You may wonder at the point of it all, and little issues like that,
- You may become totally disinterested in outside things like gossip, television, radios, newspapers, fashion, politics, the weather, tomorrow, yesterday, your friends, your family and other things that were very important before,
- You may start talking to trees and your God and they may even start to talk back.

Sometimes it's as if the whole world, as you knew it, was suddenly whipped away and you find yourself in a strange land. You are exhausted and don't have the energy to figure anything out. You simply lie there wondering what's going to happen next and what the new rules are. As you wonder, they come to you, one by one. The best you can do here is nothing. Allow the stillness. Allow the nothingness. As Spike Milligan said, "And suddenly nothing happened. Nothing did happen, but it happened suddenly." Robin Norwood (author of Why Me Why This Why Now) had a seven-year moment of stillness. Yours may not be quite as long or it may be longer – don't let anyone else tell you to "pull your socks up" or "get yourself together" or "it's about time you went back to work" or "it's time you got real" or "it's time you got off your cloud and came down to earth" or any of those other "useful things" people say to others when they feel uncomfortable that someone else is listening to their need for stillness when they are feeling guilty that they are not. You know exactly how long to stay on your cloud and, please, don't come down until you are ready. There is no prescribed incubation time – take as long as you need and don't feel any need to "get over it".

While it will feel that nothing is happening (on the outside) it is probably the most productive time for inner development and even when you cannot feel the changes within, just know that they are taking place. If you don't feel anything is happening inside, do a survey – just walk along the street or go and see some friends. Whether people say anything or not, they will notice the changes (though they won't know just what they are – you just look different, somehow!) and you will notice them noticing. Yes, the stillness is worth it for you are worth it – the world needs you and it needs you to be feeling in touch with your greater self and in touch with your greatest passion, whatever that is.

Arms and legs

By now you have thought, felt and "know'd" your way through the doorway. You've cast off some old truths and become the new ones and now it's time for action. If you've done a good job of the previous three phases, you will be eager to rush into the last phase, the one of action. It's now time to get back into the world and to express your new being.

1. Stage one required your own thought processes and, perhaps, someone as a sounding board to check your reasoning.
2. Stage two needed many more human resources in terms of emotional support.
3. Stage three needed nothing but your own self.
4. Stage four will see you looking for practical resources with which to realize your next project – friends, colleagues, new learnings, certificates, assets, experiences – resources you may never have dreamt you would ever need. Or maybe the "new" project is the same old one, with a different slant or seen with new eyes.

Whatever the direction now, there will be something new about it, even if it's just renewed vigour.

And so you do it – it's that simple! Just do it, as Nike says.

Saying "Just do it!" may be easy, but doing it may not be. Now that you're doing something, the rest of the world is going to notice. You were on the wrong track before and this time you're going to get it right, do it perfectly! Sorry, but you're probably not going to get it right. Like your first baby-steps, you'll probably stumble. And yet, you may not. Who knows until you make a move? So, in this new venture, how do you know how to make the right moves? You don't and you never will.

Get all the advice you can and then act on your own inner advice and feelings.

Yes, I said ACT – Do something. Anything is better than nothing when you feel the urge for action. You know that if you sit in your mountain cave, waiting for instructions to appear on tablets of stone, it could be a long wait – the rest of your life, maybe. "God helps those who help themselves" and the only way is for you to take a step and see how it feels. If it feels right, take another. If it didn't feel right, take a different one.

Do → feel → adjust → do → feel → adjust → do → feel → adjust → do → feel → adjust …

Comfort Zones Or Adventure?

Sitting still sometimes achieves more than activity.

Finding yourself may be done in any number of ways. People find themselves through sport, politics, business, astrology, relationships, service, religion, crime, esoteric study, scientific study, travel, isolation and countless other ways.

As you walk the long dark hallway of your soul in search of your truth, you may occasionally turn on a light to illuminate your next few steps. That light may be a psychic reading, a promotion, a new relationship, a gold medal or any of the above illuminations and it is important that they are seen and used as that – like a lamppost, they are there for illumination and not for support.

When you turn on a light you do not stare and marvel at the light bulb, but are pleased to feast your eyes on that which it illuminates. You also know that a light bulb remains fixed to the ceiling and if you were to follow it you would be going nowhere.

You're on a journey with destination unknown and the only marker posts are those illuminators you find along the way. At times they are so far apart, with large dark spaces between, that it is tempting and understandable to hold on to the last one with a fearful and trembling heart. Or you may simply hold on to it with a calmness that speaks of a need for comfort and certainty.

Staying in your comfort zone

Your needs of comfort and security must be met. If the all-knowing beings out there (friends, family and so on) are telling you to get out of your comfort zone you may, without guilt or malice, invite them into your moccasins and then ask them to speak of your needs. Your moccasins will fit no one else and, so, there is no one who can know better than you what you need to do. You need to do what you need to do and only you have your body, your mind, your beliefs, your talents, your strengths, your weaknesses, your experiences and your dreams – you are unique.

It doesn't matter how many qualifications they've got, how many experiences they've had or how much empathy they have for you, no-one knows better than you do, where to put your moccasins next. You know exactly what's right for you and you know this for every second of your life.

You may like to listen to all the advice coming your way as long as it goes over your shoulder and not up your nose – don't hook to it but allow it all to pass by, with your heart (with an "aah") choosing what's right to accept[12].

So, if you need to rest a while, do so. Feel calm, secure and content. Blob out. Enjoy the rest and quietly smile as all helpful advice passes by. By being still you may be pushing the buttons of those afraid to be still[13], and realize what a brilliant mirror you have become.

Marker posts and deserts

After a time you will know it is the moment to move from that comfort zone and make some move or other. Holding to the last illuminator, the last marker post of life direction, you may see only a barren and bleak desert ahead. That is what you see when you hold to a truth that's not yours. You now know that it is time to move on and as you let go of the marker post, the scene changes before your eyes. As you venture from certainty, from known beliefs and actions, into a space of unknowing, the desert before you will suddenly blossom into life and the sustenance you need for your next step is right there.

There is a time for stillness, a time for movement, a time for quietness, a time for adventure – only you know what the time is.

---

12 See the chapter, *Unhooking Your Memory*.
13 See the chapter, *Activity Versus Action*.

Where Did I Leave My Dream?

It might be "only a dream" but remember it's "only your life" as well – what can be more tangible or important than that?

Dreamtime recalled

We all have many thousands of dreams during our lifetimes but there is one dream that keeps recurring at different times and in different ways. This is the original dream, the one we had at birth. For when you were born, you knew exactly what you were here for, what you were meant to do in this life-time. And not only did you know exactly what to do, you knew how to achieve those things.

The trouble was that you had to get through childhood – a time of great testing. You came into this world with a dream and nothing else – you were tiny and helpless and you were cared for by these huge beings who were stronger, more intelligent and could provide everything you ever wanted – food, warmth, love, laughter and much learning. These big people were so clever you quickly grew to believe they were perfect. And in your perceived perfection of them, you believed everything they said. And much of what these monster people said or implied was that, in all things, they knew better and so you believed that. You quickly grew, in your tiny and incapable state, to know that you didn't know much at all and that you were really a very incapable being – everything you needed to have or know had to be through them, or from them.

And then they sent you to a place to learn, a place where some more big people told you important things you didn't know. Unless you remembered and believed in the things they taught you, your life would be very difficult, they said – no job, no future, no security, no prosperity and so on. Understandably, you believed them and did your best to remember the things they told you. And you believed their threats so thoroughly that your life became the one they predicted.

If you couldn't remember what they told you (especially in their tests) your life was seen by you as a failure and you were never as good as those who were good at remembering. If you remembered well in those tests, you "succeeded", perhaps believing you were better than those not so good at remembering.

And so, different groups (classes?) of people developed socially, with each group consisting of those with equivalent remembering abilities. The "brightest" ones might be in one group, the "dumbest" in another and those in between in their appropriate group.

By the time you left that learning place you believed in the superiority of others (and the inferiority of yourself) so profoundly that you then spent a long time looking for others to provide your needs of happiness, acceptance, success, love and learning. This may seem like a conspiracy but it wasn't – well, not really. Most of the people who helped to sculpt your lack of belief of self (your parents, family, friends, teachers, clergy, media and so on) knew no better themselves and were unconscious of the effect of their words and actions. Of course, there were some who did it purposely to keep you under control and you now know who they were.

And so, in a very short time, that dream and that belief in your being able to achieve it, were buried under a huge pile of beliefs and expectations from so many others. That dream never left you but it became a needle under the haystack of beliefs you had about the things you must do to please others and to succeed in their world.

However, that dream persists and pops out every now and then. At some stage in every person's life, they realize that they do indeed have some unique and original talents and wisdom, some special knowing that comes from them and not from any of those other wise and clever people. This "awakening" can happen at 12, 20, 40, 70 or any other age (everyone is different) and sometimes this "awakening" can be a very gentle and safe process, just quietly moving from reliance on others to a belief in one's self. Sometimes it can be very traumatic, with the person becoming embittered and angry at the past and the people involved.

The process can emerge quite subtly and can be as bewildering for the person concerned as the others around. Along with this awakening within, come changes in behaviour and so this person may start saying "no", may become assertive, gentle, silly, serious, quiet, noisy or something they hadn't been before. This can be terrifying, bewildering, joyful, a great relief or something else to those around – spouse, parents, children, family, friends, colleagues – depending on their own state of awakening.

And while the pattern and feelings are different for each person, depending on their state of mind and the support or otherwise that's around, there are two things that are constant:

The first is that, once started, there is no going back. The new feelings, knowings, beliefs and behaviours may be denied for a time, and hidden from friends and family for a longer time. However, the process is relentless and the inner urgings will have their way and will eventually be expressed. Bottling them up for too long is more traumatic than letting them out sooner.

The second thing is that, as the layers of others' beliefs are peeled away, the original dream is revealed with more clarity and the need to realize it becomes stronger and stronger.

Imagination, Expression, Action

Once you've uncovered this dream, what do you do with it? Well, that's entirely up to you - you have two choices:

1. Turn it into reality, or
2. Pretend it's only a dream.

Or, to quote Neale Donald Walsch's Conversations with God, "you can either go within or you can go without".

To tell yourself that "it's only a dream" is a natural first reaction and you can leave it at that if you are happy to end your life with the nagging thought of not having accomplished your full potential. Many people are content to do that but, the sort of people reading this book are unlikely to leave it at that.

There will be several questions you may now want to ask:
1. How do I know which dream is the "real" one?
2. How do I know I won't be chasing a silly fantasy?
3. What will my friends and family think of me, taking this silly/brave step?
4. How do I get people to change to let/help me to achieve the

dream?
5. What if it doesn't work out?
6. This is the real world so what am I doing chasing a dream?
7. I'm reasonably happy so why should I take this risk?
8. And even if I accept this challenge, where do I start?

And on and on your questions will pour out, with good reason. The easy and really unhelpful answer is – why not? What have you got to lose if you don't go for it?

You actually know the answer to all these questions but I will remind you. For questions 1 and 2, there are many ways to know if it is the "real" dream. If you're a scientific type you can put a blood pressure meter on your arm and think of the dream – if your pulse races when you think of it, then it's "real". If you're into radionics, then use a pendulum[14]. But, for most people, there is a simple knowing – it feels really right ... and scary, silly, illogical and all of those normal things. But it also just feels right. The acid test is to take some steps towards it and see how it feels. If you start planning it and take some positive action towards it and your enthusiasm wanes after a week, then you're on the wrong trail. However, if you find that synchronicity steps in and, somehow, things just start to help you on your way, then you're on to the "real" thing.

For questions 3 and 4, what other people think of you is none of your business – the only thing you have to change is you. Your family and friends may not be very helpful at all. When you make changes within and without, those closest to you may feel threatened by the new you. However, you will find, when you are committed, that the right people will just turn up to help. Never doubt that. It may be that you will develop new friendships and associates or it may be that your existing friends and family are very accepting. If they are, you are very lucky and don't forget to thank them.

For question 5, if it doesn't work what will you have gained? Some new insight, a new experience and a knowing about yourself.

As for question 6, where would American race relations be if Martin Luther King had not chased his dream? You know full well that realising your dream is the most "real" thing you can do – how much better off will you and the rest of humanity be if you do realize it?

For question 7, if you are so happy why are you reading this book

---

14   See the chapter, *Ideas To Try*

and all the other things you do to become more fulfilled. Not following your dream will not stop the nagging inside for change, so what gives you more fear – the fear of doing it or the fear of not ever having tried?

Three steps to heaven

Now you've nearly run out of excuses, let's see how we can do it, per question 8. In order for anything in this world to become created, there are three steps that have to be taken – imagination, expression and action or, in biblical terms, Father, Son and Holy Ghost. Before anything can be made it has to start in the mind of someone – they have to imagine it. And that is where most inventions and new ideas start – in someone's head.

How many simple inventions have you seen that you thought, "Gosh, I could have thought of that". Yes, of course you could have. The difference is that someone took the next step and expressed that thought in some way. Expression is turning that idea or dream into some form that our senses can detect and the best thing is to commit it to paper, to write it down somehow. Draw diagrams or pictures. Write a poem, song or story about it. Put something visible on paper and play with it. Some people would rather talk to someone about it and that can also work. The point is to get it out of your mind and into a more tangible form, and so having it permanently etched on paper is usually better than the spoken word.

The third and final step is to turn that "expression" into a usable object – you actually have to do something. The strange thing with this process is that if you've done the first two parts (thought and expression) thoroughly, the universe somehow steps in and does much of the doing part for you. You will find that if you take a few steps forward, help just turns up in a brilliantly synchronistic way to save you having to do it all. When you are on the right path, you are never alone.

There may, of course, be frustrations and setbacks to the plan. And as you progress you will find you are having to continually monitor and change details. However, if you hold on to that big vision, your dream will emerge. You will find that you have to be continually creative and you may be surprised at the creativity within – a creativity you never knew was there.

Whose dream am I living?

Within each and every person is a drive, or an urge, to be more than they are. Or, as someone else put it, within every human is a God-space which they then spend a lifetime trying to fill. However you term it, we have an innate desire, or curiosity, to know more, to be more than we are. And, yet, our society puts the opposite pressure on us all – to remain the same, to be "law abiding" and to not rock the boat. And so we have a battle with the inner and the outer pressures, a battle that never seems to stop.

And then we see that those people who do make a huge difference on this planet are those who do rock the boat and break the "law abiding" mould - the Mother Teresas, Nelson Mandelas, Bob Geldofs, Mahatma Gandhis, Albert Einsteins and Jesus. Our inner urge is confirmed by these people and the outer pressure to remain the same continues. The strange thing about the above rebels is that they induce change – a change that is for the benefit of society, in spite of society's objection to that change, for a while.

You also know, deep down, that if you were to realize the grandest potential of yourself, it would benefit everyone. And so your inner urges and knowings continue, while you do your best to mask them from those around you, for fear of their fears.

The hard thing is that you have to make a choice and the good thing is that, whatever choice you make, you cannot go wrong.

If you decide to stay as you are (as many do) then you stay as you are, and are safe, fed, housed, accepted and all those secure things. That is the choice of the majority of people and they continue to function effectively. There is no best or worst here – there just is, or justice.

If you decide on change, then the worst that can happen is that you could make some mistakes and learn a lot. The best is that you could:

Realize your dream,
Meet many challenging and interesting people,
Meet many challenging and interesting situations,
Receive the abundance you want,
Make many like-minded friends,
Have lots of fun doing it, and
Know you have made a large contribution to yourself and to the world.

In making that choice you can consider how you would make it if you had 24 hours to live – then one week to live and then one month. That will show you your priorities. If you had one day left to live, would you be doing what you are now? For, indeed our days are numbered and we only realize it when it's too late!

In making your decision, you have two questions:
1. Whose life am I living – mine or someone else's?
2. Do I want to die with the dreadful feeling that my fears were greater than my dreams and that I never discovered what I really enjoy?

How long can you wait till the real you emerges? Get lazy, get thought-less - it takes much less effort than being someone else.

You deserve you and so do we.

Creating Your Intentional Life

You are not here just to fill in the space between birth and death with meaningless activity. You are here, on this Earth, to fulfil some particular functions. These functions will provide two things:
1. An understanding of who you really are, and
2. Your unique gifts to the world.

As dissatisfaction with aspects of your life grows, you may begin to wonder what's happening to you. You may feel uneasy, lost, frightened, angry or many other things. You may feel that you are "losing it" and you surely are. What you are losing is that which is not you, that which does not serve you any more, that which holds you back. If you feel lost, you are already on the path to finding out who you really are.

The journey you have started has many signposts, but you may not know how to read them. This section gives you ideas and understanding about you and your new journey, which actually started many years ago. The exercises in this section will help you read the sign posts, find your passion and create a fulfilling and joyful future. This book doesn't tell what you must do, but it will help you find, within yourself, what is best for you in any given moment.

This is not a journey for the faint-hearted but it is a journey of joy, fulfilment and a realisation of your Original Intention, which is that which stirs your heart, that which you are most passionate about.

The Elephant

When a man unsheathes his pen,
The whole world knows what he's doing next.
He opens his soul and reveals his secrets,
In every paragraph and word of text.

Some call him stupid, some say brave,
But the two are the self-same thing, you see,
For stupid is what other people do,
And brave is the same damned thing, done by me.

Like the elephant that towers above the rest,
Not afraid to stand out, be seen and teach us,
This tower of strength, this determined plodder,
Is also the gentlest and kindest of creatures.

Writing a book is a long and lonely journey,
Plodding on alone, self-doubts and many restarts.
But forever is a long time, I know,
That your words will live and touch our hearts.

Many see writers as aloof, sure and intellectual,
But I see you as brave and tireless, beyond hours.
I thank you for your great message, your story,
And your inspiration of strength, oh brother of ours.

Written to my friend, David Gau-Ghan, on his 40th birthday, a week before his first book was printed – Philip.

Your Journey

I don't mind where you've been, but you're a friend if you're going my way.

As you opened this book you embarked on a journey of change. This journey is your journey and no one else's. You might like others to come along with you to share the adventure, but it's more likely that those closest to you will feel challenged or threatened by your leaving without them. They may well find a whole range of reasons for you not to read this book, to do the exercises and to make the changes that arise. There'll be things like lack of finance, lack of time and all sorts of other things you should feel guilty about – you may find that there are lots of small things that have suddenly become urgent, things that need to be done before you have time for this silly book and the things that arise from it.

Sometimes that resistant friend is yourself and you'll find all sorts of excuses to resist that which you have an urge to do.

However, no matter how hard your nearest and dearest implore you, you know that you cannot stay where you are – you must make this trip for the changes it will bring are as necessary as air and water. You can't explain why. You just have to do it. You may want to explain to your friends why you seek change but you just can't. Don't even try. You may want to justify your need for change but you don't need to. You have an urge and you are following it – unable to explain it to yourself, you'll only confuse everyone (including yourself) if you try to explain the unexplainable. You may bump into someone who's been through some change and the only explanation needed is a look – you nod to each other and you both know what's happening. Words are not only unnecessary, they are an obstruction. That is hard for those on the sideline but there is nothing you can do to help their confusion.

You may wish to tell others about your magical journey so they will join you. With evangelical fervour, you may want to convert everyone to your new way. Please resist the urge – you'll only threaten and confuse them and you'll put them off forever. Be patient and as you proceed on your journey, certain people will notice the changes in you. Their comments may surprise and delight you, and these people will be open to hearing about your journey. In them you can feel the comfort of sharing your experiences and, from them, you will receive confirmation that your journey is indeed worthwhile.

Yes, this is your journey and no one else's. Do not expect resistance and misunderstanding, but do not be surprised if you get them. That is usually the way of those who embark on the Change Journey. Do not expect to be alone but do not be surprised if you take the first few steps by yourself. That, too, is often the way. However, as you progress and change, others will join you. That is always the way.

If you happen to have a friend who is enthusiastic and passionate about starting the journey with you, you are both blessed indeed. As you travel together, be thankful for your friend's support and remember, it's still your journey. They may walk the whole way with you or they may stop and rest while your urge is to go on. Follow that urge for you do no favours to halt your progress to give pity to a friend – you halt the progress of both of you by that action.

This strange journey is one that has no reason beyond the irrepressible urge to do it. Just know that though you step out bravely into the unexplainable, the reason for your journey will unfold as you travel and, somewhere down the track, your aloneness will cease.

This is the way of all great journeys.

Exercises

1. As you contemplate or start something new, write down all the things that need to be done before you can start:

Things to do   Yes/No

....
....
....
....
....
....
....
....
....
....
....
....
....

2. Beside each item put a "yes" or a "no", depending on whether they take you closer towards or further away from your intended destination.

3. In looking at the "no" items, consider how different your life will be, in five years time, if you never do those things.

4. In looking at the "yes" items, consider whether each one really needs to be done right now. In considering each item, imagine how devastatingly different (better or worse) your life is going to be, in five years time, if it was put off for a day, a week, a month, a year or a lifetime.

5. How will your life be in five years time if you continue to do what you've always done?

Your Life Purpose

Finding the meaning of life gives meaning to our lives.

I don't know the meaning of life or why we're born – nobody does. If I was to go somewhere to find out, I couldn't come back and tell you. The only way I'll ever know the true meaning of life is to end it, to die. It's not that important for me to know!

A lot of people think they know the meaning of life. I thought that I did. But I also thought I knew the meaning of life five years ago, and it has a different meaning now compared to then … and it will probably change again, and again …

So, here we are, forced into the world, kicking and screaming, and once we get here, no one can tell us what we're meant to do or what the point of it is. Our parents, teachers, friends, priests, employers, governments and everyone else around us, make wild guesses. But nobody really knows. And so we're guided along this life path by people who really don't know where they're going (or why they're here), because they were guided by other people who didn't know where they were going (or why they were here) … and so it's gone throughout history.

We don't know why we're here so we stumble along and only find out when it's too late. All we can do with this life purpose thing is to guess or to pretend. It helps to have some idea of the reason we're here for it gives some framework for the structure of our lives. Religions recognise that such a structure is needed and they formulate their own different rules and reasons. This is helpful, but which of the many different "structures" do you choose? Perhaps it doesn't matter, for whatever purpose or intention we choose, we all get to be born, to live and to die. Different purposes, same outcomes.

The important thing to realize is that any belief is simply pretending, which is telling yourself you know something that can never be known. This is not to mock any belief, but simply to recognise that any belief can be changed, to give a similar outcome.

Some time ago I set out my belief, or pretence, in a story. The next chapter is a story – a story that fits for me. See how it feels for you.

Exercises

1. For how long have you suspected that you are on some sort of mission or that you have some sort of purpose or reason for being here?
Years ……. Months …….. Days ……. Minutes …….

2. How many people have you talked to about this? No. ………….

3. Of the people you know, how many might think like this? No. …….

How many people have told you about their feelings of a Life Purpose or Intention? Write their names

…………………………………………………………………………

…………………………………………………………………………

…………………………………………………………………………

…………………………………………………………………………

5. Why do you and/or other people not talk about this subject very much?

…………………………………………………………………………

…………………………………………………………………………

…………………………………………………………………………

…………………………………………………………………………

4. If you knew people you could share these feelings with, how would you feel?

…………………………………………………………………………

…………………………………………………………………………

…………………………………………………………………………

The Awareness System

Clever people improve things by addition – creating complexity.
Geniuses improve things by subtraction – returning to simplicity.

The universal system is difficult to comprehend, from a human perspective, for it does not punish bad deeds and it does not reward good deeds – it simply observes, benignly, knowing that all is well. Another problem is its rulelessness – without rules it is impossible to create a religion or an organisational structure that empowers a small number of power brokers to enslave the masses, as the Human System does. The Universal System (or Awareness System) is very empowering for the individual, and self-empowered individuals cannot be enslaved by fear, as is the practice of all religions. The Awareness System is very empowering for no one is actually born with Original Sin or Bad Karma or any other disadvantage. As new-born babies we are nothing but innocent perfection. Then we go through life to discover (or realise) what we really aren't, in order to discover (or become aware of) what we really are – that innocent perfection that we were in our first moment.

In order to get a feel (for the awareness system is not one you can learn with your mind – you can only know or feel it in your heart) of how the system works, we'll go back in time to when the universe began, to see how and why it got to be the way it is. None of us, of course, know the form and nature of God but we'll create a simple picture that will help you get a sense of the system. Whether this picture of God is accurate or not does not matter – what matters is that you'll know the rightness or otherwise by the feelings you get in your heart and stomach.

Imagine that God is an invisible ball of energy, ever swirling, ever pulsating. This silent, invisible, pulsing mass of creative consciousness is huge – larger than several galaxies, and whatever size your imagination can hold, let that be the size of God for you. Nothing exists in this intangible place except for an unmoving but intelligent and alive awareness. There are no people, stars, birds, traffic lights, hamburgers, houses, footballs, animals, trees or anything else – just this silent, invisible, almost-no-thing in the greater sea of no-light – not darkness but no-light. If it were possible to imagine the most utter and unimaginable peace and contentment, you would be getting close to the feeling we have here.

Over millennia of millennia there is no apparent change, such is the slow evolution, but change and evolution are indeed happening. As this mass of contented feelingness, this huge ball of intelligent consciousness grows, it starts to become aware of itself. It is contented and peaceful with what it becomes aware of. It pulses, it grows, it expands in consciousness and feelings and becomes more aware of that which it is becoming.

Then somewhere in the timelessness of its growing awareness, in the limitlessness of its size, a growing yearning begins. This speck of yearning grows slowly but, after millennia, is growing to an ache that must be heeded. This yearning is the yearning to know itself from the outside. The current awareness has been of a being inside itself and it now grows a need to see itself from outside. This need grows, an idea forms and the first tangible act of the universe is performed – this being without tangible beingness extends an aspect of itself to look back on itself, to fulfil a greater need of self-awareness.

In this process of moving from inner to outer observation there came a realisation that a different form of perception was needed. To observe the inner aspect, awareness came from simply knowing. To observe the outer aspect, different senses were needed. This intangible being could sense nothing of its outer self with its knowing senses and began to wonder how to know of its outer essence. Slowly, very slowly, did the tangible senses arise, along with tangibility itself.

From a being that was no more than pure intelligence there arose, firstly, a new mode of perception – visual perception. However, as the seeing senses developed, there came a realisation that there was nothing to see. How did one create an image to be detected by this new awareness sense? As the question was asked, the tangible pictures developed – pictures that could be sensed by this picture-sensitive perception sense. This being created images of itself, upon itself, and played with this new sense. And it wanted more ... so the senses of sound, smell, taste and touch grew ... and so did the "images" that these senses could detect. And as this mass of intelligence grew in awareness of itself, from different sense perspectives, so it smiled and played with the images that it presented to itself. And it was amused and contented. But nothing stands still and another yearning began to grow. This mass of intelligence now had colour, shape, texture, sound and odour but the yearning grew for more, for this mass of growing and changing knowingness was all there was. When there is no other, except the absence of other, when the only other is the darkness, there is nothing to know oneself as contrast to other. How did it compare? What did other look like? Was other bigger, smaller, brighter, darker, more content, less intelligent or more loving. If there is no other, how does one perceive the truth of the oneself? This yearning grew and, in time, this yearning made itself known in a need to create other, from which to compare the essence of the self. And so the tangible creation process of others began.

Some talk of the Big Bang and the Waitaha people talk of the first two comets that were sent out from consciousness – one comet of water and the other of fire, which may be the Blue Star and Halley's Comet. Whether either of these two stories are connected with this movement of expanded awareness, no one really knows, but the possibility exists. The Waitaha story tells us that the first two comets made the universe – they were sent out to create similarity and diversity. Whether it happened this way or not is not important, but in some way (probably in a way human perception cannot imagine) the first tangible other was created and more tangible others were created. And why? So the original intelligence, the first force, could expand its awareness of that which it was. No other reason. Simply to know, simply to become aware.

This original force started creating and, initially, the creations were very similar to one another but, as awareness of its creativity increased, so did its creativity and so a diverse and wondrous universe arose from the first and last question – who am I?

We are the question and the answer that we've been asking ourselves for countless millennia.

Exercises

When you think of the toys you were given as a child, which ones do you still remember and value – the simple ones like teddy bears, books and pictures or the complex, high-technology ones you couldn't fix by yourself?

....
....
....
....
....

What sort of people are you most drawn to – the ones with much drama, busyness and complications in their lives, or the ones who sail through life with grace, ease and simplicity?

....
....
....
....
....

Do you think the above preferences tell you anything about yourself – where you are now or where you want to be?

....
....
....
....
....

Our Life Purpose

Most people aim for nothing and hit it with amazing accuracy.

The essence of our life purpose is simply to find out who we really are. To do this we are presented, in every second of our lives, with reflections of who we are, in the people and circumstances that surround us. This brings an element of self-responsibility that challenges many people, but it also gives a huge measure of control over where we want to go, or to be.

Some people think that we are born, then we die and the space between should be filled with some sort of activity – any sort of activity. That is a life without purpose, without any sort of intention.

Some other people see the whole thing in black and white – good versus bad, heaven versus hell, God versus devil. In that belief is a set of rules which, if followed to the letter, will bring you to good, heaven or God. However, many of those people, while following their rules, experience bad, hell and devils on this Earth. It doesn't always seem to work, even if all the rules are followed. In fact, having to follow the rules can create so much anxiety that it doesn't feel anything like heaven. A problem with this is that there are many different sets of rules and whatever set you follow, you are not guaranteed any sort of happiness or fulfilment.

And the strange thing is that many who do not follow those rules seem to be happy and fulfilled. Are the rules wrong? This would be preposterous to contemplate as most of those rules have been around for centuries and so many peoples' lives are based on them. Have those millions of people got it all wrong? This can only be judged by the feelings of fulfilment, joy and purpose of those people. If they are completely happy, then the rules are right for them. If they're not happy, different rules might be more appropriate. The fact that there are many different sets of rules means that there is no one rule that applies to all people. The important thing is to find your rules, which might be quite different from everybody else's. As stated at the start, this is your journey and its uniqueness is your uniqueness.

Whatever belief you have surrounded yourself with, you know in your heart that, beyond all beliefs, there is an immutable reason for one thing – you! There is a reason for you. There is a reason for your existence. There is a reason for the time and place of your birth. There is a reason for the particular parents you have. There is a reason for every person and experience you have ever encountered. There is a reason you're reading this book.

The reason is that you have a mission. The reason is that you have a definite and unique purpose for being here. The reason is that you entered this life with an Intention – an intention to achieve something for yourself and an intention to give your special gifts to the world. When you let this intention lapse, you see and feel less of good, of heaven and of God. When you take up the challenge of that intention, when you listen to the whisperings of your heart, you become empowered, enlivened and fulfilled. When you follow that Original Intention, the world benefits beyond measure from your gifts.

Sadly, most people remain in doubt. Most people remain in ignorance of that Intention and are afraid to reconnect with it. You see, the design was that you were to come into this world with a knowing of that Intention, you were then to forget it and, later, remember it. You were presented with people and experiences that took you as far from that Intention as possible. At some stage, you were meant to say, "Enough!" At some stage, you were pushed far enough away that you just had to stop, turn around and start on your way back home to that Intention. Most people do not recognise that there is an Intention, there is a reason and that there can, indeed, be good, heaven and God.

Only a few have the courage to say, "Enough!" Only a few realise their great gifts and look for ways to pursue that Intention. Only a few have the courage to say, "I'm lost and I want to find my way home. Where is it?" You are one of those few. You are one of the courageous ones who have remembered that there is, indeed, an Intention. You may not know what it is, but you know it's there. To know that you're lost means that you know that, somehow, there's a way out and there's a way home. Admitting that you're lost or confused is the first step to becoming found. You are one of the few who are about to find your way home. You are one of the few who are going to carry out their Intention. You are going to make a difference in this world.

You started with your Intention firmly embedded in your soul. Then the people and experiences in your life successfully covered it with rules, obligations and ideas that go against your Original Intention. This is what usually happens. But this Original Intention was never forgotten – it was simply buried under the debris of that which your society insisted you must learn. So, having said, "Enough!" you've taken your first step and we celebrate your rebirth.

The next step is the one most people do not take. They continue a life without intention, a life that others have designed for them, a life without meaning. For them, good, heaven and God are nice, fluffy concepts that aren't real. For you, they're very real, though you don't actually know what shape this "real" is. You're on your way.

The best way to clean poisoned or unhealthy water is to run it through verbiloforms (the biodynamic way) or through something like the Grander System, which creates turbulence and a particular pattern in the water which, in turn, helps the water to recall and become its originally pure state. Taste this water and you'll know it's healthy! Does the water's turbulence and recalling of what it originally was, remind you of your own situation of late?

If you want to clean your windscreen, you don't add anything to it. On the contrary, you simply take dirt away. Your education consisted of adding dirt to the naturally beautiful and clear glass that you are. The journey home is simply unlearning that which has clouded your vision. Only by unlearning can you come to a true understanding of who you really are. Only by washing the windscreen of your soul will you ever see, with complete clarity, your Original Intention and your Reason for Being. Before this moment of admitting to being lost, your life may have been like mine ...

Exercises

1. Think of the people you know who have very busy and complicated lives – do they emanate a great inner peace and an inner knowing of who they really are?

....
....
....
....
....
....

2. Think of the people you know who are totally spontaneous and uninhibited - do they emanate a great inner peace and an inner knowing of who they really are?

....
....
....
....
....
....

3. Do you relish your quiet moments or are you afraid of silence and being still?

....
....
....
....
....
....

Learning To Be Me

In learning and unlearning the rules of our teachers, we finally come to know who we really are.

Once upon a time there was a boy called John whose greatest lesson in life was that he was not good enough. One day he rushed home from school and excitedly told his mother about how he had come top of his class in a French test and he had got 98%. His mother's only comment was, "So what did you do wrong with the 2%?" His perception was that whatever he did, it was never good enough and he came to expect condemnation for everything he did.

This boy became my father.

The way he perceives it, he was the little golden boy until he was seven – up to that age he could do nothing wrong and his sister could do nothing right. Then, for no apparent reason, the system was reversed and from seven onwards he could do nothing right and his sister could do nothing wrong. We all remember, as children, that whenever we were to visit our grandmother, we would take bets on who would be the favourite – one of us would get more sweets, gifts and compliments, while the other three might not actually receive any of those things.

The important point here is that my father perceived his childhood to be very unhappy, while his sister (2 years younger) sees her childhood as very happy. It doesn't matter what our parents (and other people) actually do; it is what we perceive they do that shapes our attitudes and behaviour.

So John, who learned he was never good enough, spent the rest of his life trying to be perfect. He passed his Grand Lesson on to me and I learned it very well for my first forty years. With Dad's need for perfection, he wouldn't try anything new unless he knew that he could do it perfectly. If he was making something, he would always do it alone so no one would see anything until the perfect final product was proudly displayed. From this I believed that everything I wanted to do, I had to do alone and I never learned to work cooperatively. During my first marriage my wife and I bought, renovated and sold four houses and I did all the renovations (building, plumbing, electrical work, painting, wallpapering, roofing, concreting etc.) myself. I was very proud of this but there was a cost – there was less time for my family as I worked every evening and weekend to create yet another perfect result for the world to admire.

Also, when I made something, Dad would immediately trash (verbally, physically or both) my childish creation and off he'd go, make the perfect thing and proudly bring it back for me. I learned that I was not competent at creative things. I unlearned this when I started renovating houses!

My father's need for perfection meant that he focussed on results and the cost of getting them didn't matter. On the 22,000-acre farm that he managed, being able to ride a horse was a matter of survival and so from around four years old I had to learn. I wasn't allowed a saddle until I was able to ride properly (at about seven years) and until then I sat on a sheepskin, strapped to the horse. One hot day, after starting out at 5.00 am and mustering all day, we returned home at about 5.00 pm, hot and exhausted. As we got home, Dad decided that it was time his five-year-old son learned to gallop on a horse. So he made me gallop up and down the gravel driveway and every time I fell off, he forced me back on the horse to "get it right". He would not let me give up until I had galloped along this 100-metre driveway, in shorts and t-shirt, at least four times without falling off. After falling off about six times I made it and, bleeding all over, went crying to Mum who was aghast at her little wounded son. She put me in a hot bath and gave me some chocolate – it's funny the things we remember! I learned from this, and many other instances, that learning was necessarily painful and hard work – it was never fun.

My father's thorough teaching meant that the things he taught me will never be forgotten – killing sheep, riding horses, shoeing horses, mustering sheep, lambing ewes[15], driving vehicles, giving injections to

---

15   Helping sheep to give birth to their lambs

animals, setting the table, cooking meals, polishing shoes – all things, great and small. For example, to learn how to back a trailer, I had to back for hours (it seemed) along winding gravel roads until I could hardly move my neck – it was sore for the next week! However, this skill served me well as an army driver and in many other situations.

I was thankful for his thorough training but I do wish he had also taught me that it was O.K. to make mistakes once in a while – I had to unlearn perfection and then teach myself that imperfection is sometimes alright, and that process took three times as long to learn as it took to learn the original "perfection" lesson from my father.

Looking back from today's perspective, I feel the greatest lesson I learned from my parents was about the denial of expression. My father had very strong views on every subject and no one was allowed to question or challenge anything. My siblings and I (and maybe Mum too!) were all terrified of this large, dominating man and it was to my constant detriment that I was born with a mind that needed to know everything – I could not accept opinions or anything else at face value and I wanted to know the why and wherefore of every atom and action in the universe.

I might ask why we had to cut the tails off the lambs as it seemed so cruel and Dad would patiently explain that their tails got caked in their faeces and so I'd ask, "Why don't we give them a diet that doesn't give them constant diarrhoea – why don't we grow other grasses and herbs for them to eat?" and he'd angrily say that ryegrass and clover were the best pasture for this country. I'd ask, "why?" and be told not to ask such "bloody stupid questions" and this might be accompanied with a whack from his hand, a stick or whatever was nearby. But my inquisitive mind would have to know the answer and so I'd try to pick an opportune moment to continue the questions about grass, fertilizers, politics, religion or whatever, and it would invariably end in him yelling at me and hitting me again. I soon learned to transcend the physical pain but the denial of my own curiosity just made me want to know and question more. As my repression and anger grew, my belief in myself died. I learned to say, "yes" to most things, even when I didn't agree. I learned that my opinion and knowledge (and, therefore, myself) were of no value and I learned that questioning and confrontation always ended in pain and humiliation.

Years later my wife reminded me that I had had eleven jobs in the last ten years – every time there was a disagreement, I backed off and ran away to another job, rather than face the possible pain and humiliation of the disagreement.

During my childhood, any emotional expression was squashed. We were forbidden from talking or making any noise at the table (which made it very difficult when we got the giggles!) and I was not allowed to cry – if I did, I would be told to, "Stop it or I'll give you something to cry about!" This meant another belting if the crying didn't stop in a few seconds. Equally, any positive expressions of joy or happiness were frowned upon and we were told not to be so silly, stupid or childish. I learned that there was a very narrow range of allowable emotional expression. This effectively shut the door to my emotions and I only relearned to cry at the age of forty. Often I would feel really bad but I had no idea what that "badness" was about – the badness, coupled with the frustration of not knowing why it was there, would bring out the worst of my anger, which my wife and children had to bear. Then one of my most ecstatic moments happened in 1993 when I was driving along (I still remember the exact spot!) and I felt one of these "badness" clouds descend on me. For some reason I put my right hand on my stomach and, for the first time in my life, I had a word for the "badness". I don't remember if it was loneliness, sadness, feeling abandoned or what, but in spite of the negative feeling, I felt so incredibly alive in being able to identify a feeling.

My mother also taught me to keep my mouth shut. She was such a social person and, being very proud of her children, would tell the whole neighbourhood about every little thing we did. This was fine for Geoff, my outgoing and gregarious brother but for me (the shyest child in the universe) it was absolute hell. I quickly learned to tell Mum nothing about my life, though I sometimes forgot. Near the end of my first marriage I asked Mum and Dad if they could look after our children for two days to give us some space to sort out our problems – I made Mum promise not to tell anyone else in their town about our failing marriage. Two weeks later we visited Mum and Dad and several people in the street offered their condolences on our personal problems. I confronted Mum about this and she said, "Oh, I only told Joan about it." Joan was the town gossip!

The last big lesson came when I went to boarding school. I was there from the age of eleven to eighteen and during that time I excelled in almost everything I did. I represented my college at more sports than anyone else and that record still stands today. Unfortunately, prizes were only awarded for specialists and us all-rounders went unrecognised. I was very proud of my achievements and always wanted Dad to see me playing sport – he never did as he was always too busy working. I think Mum saw one athletics day and one rugby game. Then the final blow came when I was fourteen – Mum and Dad had got themselves into a financial mess and Mum told me that from now on they would pay for my schooling and food and there'd always be a free room at home for me. If I needed anything else though, I would have to pay for it myself. It felt like the bottom had fallen out of my world and, in great terror, I started ringing the neighbours to see if they had any work for me during the holidays. Luckily, one of them did. This perceived lack of interest and support in my life added to my great feeling of aloneness and it took another twenty years before I was able to trust people and to have healthy friendships, especially with men.

Mum and Dad were not bad people. Dad thought he was teaching me to "do things right" (meaning his way) and because of his inability to be seen to be imperfect, was unable to admit to not knowing something or admit to accepting that someone (especially a child of his) may have some wisdom or ideas that he didn't. His only way of defending his vulnerable spots was with anger. He knew no other way and he simply reacted in the time-honoured way that men have been taught to – by lashing out. In fact, Dad was a very caring man – if he hadn't cared so much he wouldn't have been so meticulous in giving me useful life skills.

Mum never tried to hurt me – she was a gregarious and social person who was so proud of her children and she was unable to understand the shyness I had then.

I learned to behave the way my parents wanted me to and repressed the true me. This led to a lot of resentment, anger and hatred towards them. As a young adult I tried to change them and get them to see things my way – perhaps unconsciously trying to do to them what they had done to me. However, I eventually learned to forgive them and accept them as they were. As I came to realise that they were not bad people, but simply doing the best that they knew how, with the skills they had, I was able to release the hold they had over me – I was able to unlearn the lessons I didn't like and I was able to really appreciate the good lessons I received from them. My love and appreciation of them has grown immeasurably from accepting their imperfect humanness.

My upbringing has a similar ring to that of so many other people of my generation that I talk to. Many of our parents liked things to be neat and tidy, with obedience, conformity and predictability being paramount. Many of our parents' age see the present world as falling apart and out of control and their answer to that is to exert more control with more laws, "policemen", and denial. However, my generation see the celebration of diversity, individual expression and experimentation as a really positive expansion of who we are and who we can be. Often, our answer to a problem is not to bottle it but to release it, express it and to accept it.

My parents and I are not different from others of our respective generations – we are perfect mirrors of our time and the only things that separate us are the ways we look at the world. Perception is probably the only thing that separates anyone.

And so, from the ashes comes the phoenix – from the shyest boy with the greatest suppression of spirit and expression (that's my perception and I'm sticking to it!) comes a man who makes his living by writing books, running workshops and singing – a life more filled with public expression than I could ever have imagined. If I had not been battered about and squashed (emotionally) I doubt if I would have had the passion I now do for helping people find their passion, their true selves and their true calling.

I needed to go (or be led) down the wrong path in order to find my right path. There comes a time in everyone's life to say, "Enough!" There comes a time in everyone's life to choose their own path. Not everyone makes these choices but the opportunities are always there. From observation, most people stay on the uncomfortable but familiar lane, simply because it is familiar. As we come to the roundabouts of life we must choose whether to change lanes or not.

After ten years of accounting I was made redundant and, though I wasn't keen on it by then, I chose to stay with it. I was made redundant again and, though I disliked accounting more by then, I took another accounting job. The third time I was made redundant, I was beginning to see the light[16] – I decided the universe didn't want me to be an employee so I started my own accounting practice. Though I absolutely

---

16 Some people make the change when they see the light, some wait till they can feel the heat.

loathed accounting by then, I pretended everything was great while my accounting practice wasn't.

Eventually I gave up and said, "I don't know what to do. Please give me some help ... anyone!" Finally, I was sincere and passionate enough to be ready for change and, within a month, I was teaching at the local Polytechnic. That started me down a completely different path but there still something missing, I felt. With passion and sincerity I started listening to my gut feelings and the illogical thought of not working nagged at me. Eventually I gave in to this "not working" idea (something I hadn't done since I was fourteen) and went to Australia and wandered for three months. I returned with quite a different view of the world and was presented with the idea of publishing a book. I knew nothing about publishing but it seemed a good idea at the time and so I did it. I lost a lot of money over it but I learned so much and met so many interesting people that I continue doing that today. That led me to writing my own books and, with the teaching experience, I now communicate with people in a variety of ways.

I could have continued accounting (as many people suggest I should to help my finances) but I know that if I didn't listen to the gentle nudges from the universe, they would have become less gentle and the results more painful. I see this with many people who unwillingly continue in unhealthy jobs, relationships and other life situations and, as they go on, their ulcers, heart attacks, cancer, depression and other health problems grow worse. Their body will always have the last say. If they're wise and brave, they will start asking themselves some questions, like:

What's it all about?
What am I doing wrong?
How do I get myself out of this rut[17]?
Is there another way?
Is it possible to live in happiness?
Is abundance really possible?
Where can I start making changes to improve things?

The questions are really simple ones and you don't have to be a genius to ask them – you simply need a little courage, possibly mixed with some exasperation. Sincerity and passion also help.

The best advice to give is that if you're in a rut, stop digging.

---

17 A rut is a grave with the ends kicked out

When you don't know what to do, do nothing. Find ways of avoiding people, especially those who are prone to giving advice. The only advice you need at this time is your own and solitude is a great way of finding it.

There are many ways of ensuring minimal contact with others:

Let your grass grow so they'll think you're away	Just listen
Embarrass people so they'll stay away	Speak very slowly
Sit under a tree	Hide
Wear underwear on the outside	Walk backwards
Send out change-of-address forms and stay home	Change your name
Sell your phone, television and letterbox	Just sit
Wear disguises and pretend to talk in Mongolian	Laugh
Hide your car at your neighbour's place	Smile benignly
Wear a hearing aid and pretend you're deaf	Cry
Paint your face and say you have leprosy	Have a holiday
Take your pet banana for a walk, on a lead	Talk to your trees
Get a guard dog	Act invisible
Tell people how you're really feeling when they ask	Do hand-stands
Walk around with your mouth open	Say you're a politician

The first impulse, when you're in trouble, is to get your answer from someone else[18]. Sorry, but your training has got you into trouble again, for the best advice is your own and nobody has ever told you about that. If you're tempted to go and do something, ask yourself this question:

"If I do nothing today, what part of the universe will be forever damaged?"

---

18   See the chapter, *Love Is All There Is*

Exercises

1. When you're asked to do something you don't want to do, do you:
☐ Say "yes" grudgingly,
☐ Say "yes" and pretend great joy,
☐ Say "no" and feel guilty,
☐ Say "no" and feel alright, or
☐ Other ……………………………...

2. Do you feel guilty when you do nothing or have a rest? How do you justify it when you take a break?

………………………………………………………………..…………………

………………………………………………………………..…………………

………………………………………………………………..…………………

………………………………………………………………..…………………

………………………………………………………………..…………………

………………………………………………………………..…………………

………………………………………………………………..…………………

3. Whose life are you living?

………………………………………………………………..…………………

………………………………………………………………..…………………

………………………………………………………………..…………………

………………………………………………………………..…………………

………………………………………………………………..…………………

………………………………………………………………..…………………

………………………………………………………………..…………………

………………………………………………………………..…………………

Waking Before You Die

*What is this life for if not to awaken ourselves –
how can we do that with our minds closed?*

This whole process of bumping into obstacles, recovering, crashing into walls, recovering, tripping over potholes, recovering, falling down mine-shafts, recovering … ad nauseum … can go from six months, to twenty years to whole lifetimes. Some people are faster learners than others.

Many (if not most) people spend their lives pursuing careers, relationships and activities that give them no comfort or joy. Being too frightened to step off the known, dead-end path, they become sleep walkers. Becoming fearful of parent-substitutes who might spank them, they follow the mindless routine and conflicting rules of everybody else. They fill the gnawing hole in their soul by living vicariously through the imagined or real achievements and sensations of those courageous enough to risk failure, challenge society's rules and follow their hearts.

Yes you, Dear Reader, are one of those few who will help to fulfil the empty-souled – their passive eyes will feast upon your achievements and your failures and, who knows, you may even inspire some to wake up before they die, remember their Original Intention and attempt to recapture it.

This is not the reason for your new journey, but it is a wonderful by-product of it.

As your awakening begins, you will recognise many sleepers and, with great compassion, you'll want to awaken them. You'll want others to know, feel and see what you do and so you'll nudge, cajole, enthuse, convince and generally pester them to open their real eyes ... and ... they continue snoring. In spite of all your wonderful news, they don't want to or cannot hear it, so they continue their unfulfilling jobs, unhealthy relationships and unhelpful beliefs and they curl up, in every spare moment, and give themselves to the hypnotic gaze of the lie machine – sometimes called the television.

I'm sorry, but don't bother shaking them. No matter how hard you try, you're wasting your time and you don't have much to waste. If you get any reaction it won't be positive – they'll wonder what's wrong with you, what you've been smoking, what you've just won or who you've been meeting – no one in their world can feel and emanate so much passion and enjoyment as you are, so you're obviously faking it or you're on an artificial high.

You're actually on different planets now, and there's no way you can explain about the different vegetation, atmosphere and people on yours – they just won't get it, so forget it.

However hard you try, you'll never be able to explain the smell of a sunrise, the colour of a sparrow's song, the taste of a smile, the feel of a bee's hum or the exquisite sound of a rainbow. For, truly, you will experience these things – every sensory organ will awaken and sense things in a more expansive way. The trees will be greener, the birds will sound happier, books will look wiser, holding hands will feel deeper, making love will be more profound, you will see all twelve colours in rainbows, people will appear happier and sadder and tears and laughter will roll from you in the blink of an eye. Everything will become clearer, sharper and more distinct and, yet, more connected too.

The sparrow's song will be your heart's song, the rainbow will be the colours in your eyes, the rain will be your inner cleansing, your child's hand will hold your inner child's hand and, together, you'll skip through life. Everything outside will mirror what's inside and what you sense on the inside will be sensed around you, on the outside.

None of this can be explained to a walking sleeper. Explanations can only come through words, and words cannot give full (or any) meaning to the wholeness and beauty of your expanded awareness and experience. As you try to explain these things in words, you will realise that your words actually get in the way of what you're trying to express. Words will actually debase that which you have experienced – you'll feel a little less and your listeners will feel a little confused.

As you step back into your silence and leave them to their slumbers, you may find that some will approach and wonder what's happened to you. They'll tell you that you look so much younger, so much more vibrant, so much more peaceful, so much more sexy, so much more ... well ... everything! They'll genuinely want to know what you've been up to and you'll try your best to explain with the inadequate words you have. However, despite the limitations of your words, if your friends are awakening from their slumber, they'll understand your meaning. You can answer their questions simply and honestly. However, remember you're not trying to sell anything – you're there to help them awaken and become who they really are and, from your own experience, you'll know that can be a slow process. It serves no one for you to be trying to speed them up. Firstly, if you give them lots of advice and information, you'll probably scare them back into their shell, forever. Secondly, if you boast about your new-found and great knowledge, they'll soon wonder about you as they learn other stuff and pass you on Personal Growth Road.

If you attempt to steer them in your particular direction, at your particular speed, just realise that you're creating, for them, the very situation you're trying to extract yourself from. Their path will not be yours. The best advice you can give is your silence – just listen as much as you can. When they insist on an answer don't tell them what to do but tell them what you might do in a similar situation. Then they can use your experience as one of several options to choose from. You'll also find that, as you allow them their own speed and direction, they'll appreciate your lack of pressure and judgement and they'll return – you'll have a friend for life.

You cannot go out and convert people – they must come to you, asking for help in the conversion process they've started by themselves.

Exercises
1. Think of your closest friends – do they:
☐ lecture,
☐ advise
☐ listen
☐ other...

....

2. When you have a problem, do you find the answer best by:
- ☐ talking to others about it
- ☐ working it out by yourself
- ☐ analysing it
- ☐ forgetting about it and the answer just comes, some time later

☐ other..

....

3. When someone tells you their problems, is your first impulse to:
- ☐ tell them what to do
- ☐ ask if they want any helpful ideas
- ☐ listen

☐ other..

....

4. When someone asks your advice, do you:
- ☐ tell them what to do,
- ☐ tell them what you might do, or
- ☐ give them several options or ideas

☐ other..

....

Whose Life Is It, Really?

We are all so different – just like everyone else.

Although I had believed that I was in control of my life, it came as a shock to realise that all of my decisions had been made by my parents.

You might think you are a grown, mature adult, making decisions based on what's best for you. Sorry, but many of the decisions you think you're making are actually being made by your parents, grandparents and other ancestors – whether they're alive or not.

There was a newly married young man who asked his wife why she cut the neck off the turkey before she roasted it.

"Oh, I don't know," she replied. "That's what my mother always did."

Two days later, his mother-in-law was around for a coffee and he asked her why she chopped the neck of the turkey off.

"Oh, I don't know," she replied. "That's what my mother always did."

Wanting an answer to his question, he suggested to his wife that they visit her grandmother the next weekend. She agreed and, over a cup of tea, he asked the older lady why she chopped off the neck of the turkey.

"Oh, I don't know," she replied. "That's what my mother always did."

Still determined to get to the bottom of this question, he persuaded his wife to visit her great grandmother the following weekend. His new wife readily agreed as she loved the old lady. Over a brandy, the young man asked the sprightly old lady why she chopped off the neck of the turkey before she roasted it.

"Why, it's very simple, young man," she said with a smile. "If I didn't chop off the neck, it wouldn't fit into my little oven."

Four generations later, the ovens have got larger and the turkeys are smaller, but we still act as if nothing has changed.

Another example is our schooling:

Before the Industrial Revolution, farmers had one or two house cows for their domestic milk. With the revolution, large factories started up and more people started living in towns, with fewer people having cows. Many of the remaining farms took on a factory look, having many more cows, with the milk now being sold. The factories needed people to run them and, very quickly, the factory owners realised that they needed people who were able to read and write (at a basic level) and to be able to follow routines and obey instructions. This was the start of modern schooling – children were taught the basics of reading, writing and arithmetic, as well as how to conform to strict rules. Children were cheaper than adults so it was decided that all children should attend school – this would guarantee a good supply of compliant, "educated" and cheap labour. Because many of the children were needed to help with milking, morning and evening, schools started at 9.00 am and finished at 3.00 pm. If this had not happened, dairy farmers would not have allowed their children to attend these new schooling places. It was also decided that, to "educate" these children, they had to be started at school as soon as possible, while they were still open to indoctrination. However, schools didn't want to bother with changing nappies, providing food, teaching basic speech and all those other baby needs, so five years old was chosen for the time to start school. Five was the best age for the "educators" – young enough to indoctrinate and old enough to be convenient.

The Industrial Revolution is well and truly over but we still send our children to school at around five years old and the school hours are still 9.00 to 3.00 – despite the fact that very few of them have to milk cows any more. And, despite the fact that factories have become offices with calculators, computers and spell-checkers, schools are still churning out the "factory fodder" with an emphasis on the 3 R's – reading, 'riting and 'rithmetic. The times have changed but our schooling hasn't.

For example, our teachers are still telling us that the sun is extremely hot, when we know that it isn't. If you get into your spacecraft, fly halfway to the sun and get out in your bra and nickers, you'll die of the cold in a few seconds. In fact, the sun has no temperature – it's not hot or cold – it simply emits a powerful, temperature-less energy which, when combined with our atmosphere (like sulphur combined with water) creates the heat we all feel.

With the growth of the global village, we need entrepreneurs, lateral thinkers and leaders who can work in cooperation with others for the common good. But instead, our schools are teaching adherence, subservience and competition.

Two examples[19] will show how fast we are changing:

Firstly, in Roman times, life expectancy was around twenty-five years, so Romans could live and die without experiencing any major changes in their lives. In the Middle Ages, life expectancy had risen to around fifty years, so in this time period a person would perhaps witness one major change (a war or a new king/queen) in their lifetime. By the end of last century, life expectancy had increased to three score years and ten, and people could now expect to experience three or four major social changes in their lives. My grandmother, for example, saw the advent of the motorcar and was alive to witness the first man walk on the moon! In the twenty first century we can expect to experience a minimum of four major social changes per year – what David Vice, vice-chairman of Telecom North (USA), calls the nanosecond culture.

Roman times → Middle ages	1600 years	0 → 1 change
Middle Ages →1900	300 years	1 → 4 changes
1900 → 2000	100 years	4 → 240 changes

The change is certainly accelerating!

The second example is that, in this world of high technology, no one has any product or service a competitor won't have very soon. In the 1960s or 70s a product or service could give an organisation a competitive edge for two to three years; in the 1990s that edge was nearer three to four months. In this decade that edge is being cut to two to three days!

So why are we stuck in the past? Some of the answers come from our method of bringing ourselves into the world ...

---

19   From *Shift Your But* by Ann Andrews, published by Ann Andrews, NZ, 1997.

Exercises

Write a list of the technological changes you've witnessed to date, e.g. travel, communications, medicine, housing, computers etc.

....

....

....

....

....

....

Write a list of the social changes you've witnessed to date, e.g. politics, laws, acceptance of homosexuality etc.

....

....

....

....

....

....

How often do you talk or think of the "good old days"?

....

....

Write a list of the things you have fears or concerns about in our world.

....

....

....

....

....

....

Becoming Your Parents

Children become parents to themselves.
Adults become friends to their children.

We may want to live our own lives, free of others' influence, but it just seems so hard to be us. Why is it so hard to know what's right for us and then to follow our heart? It may help to go back a day or two to our birth and recall our growing up process.

We all have many thousands of dreams during our lifetimes but there is one dream that keeps recurring at different times and in different ways. This is the original dream, the one we had at birth. For when you were born, you knew exactly what you were here for, what you were meant to do in this lifetime. And not only did you know exactly what to do, you knew how to achieve it.

The trouble was that you had to get through childhood – a time of great testing. You came into this world with a dream and nothing else – you were tiny and helpless and you were cared for by these huge beings who were stronger, more intelligent and could provide everything you ever wanted – food, warmth, love, laughter and much learning. These big people were so clever you quickly grew to believe they were perfect. You believed everything they said. And much of what these monster people said or implied was that, in all things, they knew better, and so you believed that. You quickly grew, in your tiny and helpless state, to know that you didn't know much at all and that you were really a very incapable being – everything you needed to have or know had to be through them, or from them.

And then they sent you to a place to learn, a place where some more big people told you important things you didn't know. Unless you remembered and believed the things they taught you, your life would be very difficult, they said – no job, no future, no security, no prosperity and so on. Understandably, you believed them and did your best to remember the things they told you. And you believed their statements so thoroughly that your life became the one they predicted:

If you couldn't remember what they told you (especially in their tests) your life was seen by you as a failure and you were never as good as those who were good at remembering. If you remembered well in those tests, you "succeeded", perhaps believing you were better than those not so good at remembering.

And so different groups (classes?) of people developed socially, with each group consisting of those with equivalent remembering abilities. The "brightest" ones might be in one group, the "dumbest" in another and those in between in their appropriate group.

By the time you left that learning place you believed in the superiority of others (and the inferiority of yourself) so profoundly that you then spent a long time looking for others to provide your needs of happiness, acceptance, success, love and learning. This may seem like a conspiracy but it wasn't – well, not really. Most of the people who helped to sculpt your lack of belief of self (your parents, family, friends, teachers, clergy, media and so on) knew no better themselves and were unaware of the effect of their words and actions. Of course, there were some who did it purposely to keep you under control and you now know who they were.

And so, in a very short time, that dream and that belief in your being able to achieve it, were buried under a huge pile of beliefs and expectations from so many others. That dream never left you but it became a needle under the haystack of beliefs you had about the things you must do to please others and to succeed in their world.

However, that dream persists and pops out every now and then. At some stage in every person's life they realise that they do indeed have some unique and original talents and wisdom, some special knowing that comes from them and not from any of those other wise and clever people. This "awakening" can happen at 12, 20, 40, 70 or any other age (everyone is different), and once it starts, there is no going back.

Sometimes this "awakening" can be a very gentle and safe process, just quietly moving from reliance on others to a belief in one's self. Sometimes it can be very traumatic, with the person becoming embittered and angry at the past and the people involved.

People often think the process is kick-started by serious illness, accident, redundancy, divorce or some other traumatic event. However, if we look a little deeper, we usually see that the traumatic, "outside" event was triggered by a more subtle change within. This inner change will seldom have a tangible reason for happening and it can be as bewildering for the person concerned as the others around. Along with this awakening within, come changes in behaviour and so this person may start saying "no", may become assertive, gentle, silly, serious, quiet, noisy or something they haven't been before. This can be terrifying, bewildering, joyful, a great relief or something else to those around – spouse, parents, children, family, friends, and colleagues – depending on their state of awakening.

And while the pattern and feelings are different for each person, depending on their state of mind and the support or otherwise that's around, there are three things that are constant:

The first is that, once started, there is no going back. The new feelings, knowings and beliefs may be denied for a time, and hidden from friends and family for a longer time. However, the process is relentless and the inner urgings will have their way and will eventually be accepted and expressed. Bottling them up for too long is more traumatic than letting them out.

The second thing is that, as the layers of others' beliefs are peeled away, the original dream is revealed with more clarity and the need to realise it becomes stronger and stronger.

The third is that it is impossible to make just one change. There may be a need for a physical change (eating less, eating different food, exercise, beauty treatment), a social change (wanting to meet different people, wanting to see no people, wanting to see more people) a mental change (new studies, learning new skills, joining something like Toastmasters) or a spiritual change (joining meditation classes, going to church, reading different books, meeting different people). Whatever the first small change, it will not be the only change. A desire for less meat in your diet may lead to a desire to learn more about nutrition, which may lead you to study Eastern philosophies, which may mean some meditation classes. Or a desire to improve your speaking skills may lead you to personal development workshops, which may encourage you to have some counselling, which may lead you to a study of counselling or psychology, from which you may see a better future than in your job or marriage and you leave. And, all the while, you will be meeting different people, learning about different ways of living, and thinking and feeling quite differently about all aspects of life. You cannot make one change and expect that it will stop there. Once you start, you will always want to move onto another and another and another ...

These different feelings can be both worse and better (at different times) than before, and the above changes (like a new suit) won't always feel comfortable at first. As you get used to one new suit, you'll want to try another ... and another ... and another, and you'll start experiencing life as a series of slightly uncomfortable but exciting moments.

As Mario Andretti, famous racing driver, says, "If you begin to feel you're in control, you're not going fast enough."

Exercises
1. What are your parents' beliefs about money? For example, do they think:
❐ money is difficult to make,
❐ money is easy to make,
❐ you have to work hard for money,
❐ there's never enough money,
❐ wealthy people are not to be trusted,
❐ poor people are lazy.
❐ Other ………………………………………………………………..

2. What are your beliefs about money?

3. What are your parents' spiritual/religious beliefs?

4. What are your spiritual/religious beliefs?

5. Is there something you have especially strong views about? e.g. health, sex, money, spirituality, morals, conservation, politics etc.

6. If so, is this particular subject one that your parents have very different perspectives on?

Changing Our Water

Gaining more "valuables" or gaining yourself – which do you choose?

Not only is our outer environment changing[20], but the call from inside is whispering (rather loudly!) that it's time to change. We have an idea why it's hard to separate from our roots[21]. but why are we not recognizing that the wave we're surfing is accelerating? Simply because we are the wave. We're in it, co-creating it and we're often not aware of our environment because it has always "just been there". If you ask a fish to describe water, it probably can't – it may not even realize that water even exists for it has always "just been there".

Not able to see the trees for the forest, we're unaware of the weeds, new species and fallen trees in our forest. For example, we see young men committing suicide (especially in New Zealand which has the highest rate of young male suicide in the world) at a greater rate than any other group and we wonder what's wrong with them. Maybe there's nothing wrong with them at all. Maybe, just maybe, they're the "new wave", with a consciousness ahead of the masses, in tune with their environment and they're battling the masses who are trying to force them into the Old World mould that they've long ago outgrown.

And, in your own body and mind, you have stirrings of a New World, a different way and a better life. If you try to express these things to others, you're told "you're daft", "it will never work" or "just silly flights of your imagination". And so, for a while, you believe your detractors from the Old World and you bury your imagination and

---

20   See the chapter, *Whose Life Is It, Really?*
21   See the chapter, *Becoming Your Parents*

dreamings while you get on with growing up, becoming sensible and bowing to conformity.

But where has that conforming and denial got you – more of good, heaven and God? More of love? Gosh no! It's got you more confused and frustrated and the beauty and strength you saw in yourself has withered.

So you battle with what's important. Do you get sensible, logical and normal, earning acceptance and approval from those around you? Or do you start listening to those subtle whispers from your soul, the ones that hint of a wild and free spirit inside, an expansive and joyful future that's possible and a group of enthusiastic and supportive friends, waiting around the corner for you.

Yes, it's a frightening prospect to be flinging yourself into the void, making changes with uncertain outcomes and leaving the well-trodden, predictable road behind. Are you frightened or uncertain? Well done, for if there is no adrenalin to stir you, no nerves to give you edge and no passion to awaken you, you're on the well-trodden, predictable road – the road that leads to nowhere. Only when you start walking your own unique path will your mind and body sharpen and awaken itself, and that quickening may be felt as fear or confusion.

It's like a cut on your finger – there is pain and that pain is your body's way of saying, "Please treat this finger gently". The fear and uncertainty is your body's way of saying that you are now to be more alert.

On the straight and familiar road there was security, certainty and lack of passion. However, as you take what seems to be a minor side-road, you'll be called to start using your senses as never before. On this unfamiliar and twisting road to the New World, you'll be asked to call on knowings, talents and skills you've had since the most ancient time, buried so deeply in your soul that you forgot they were there. What you call "fear" is simply your amazingly intelligent body saying, "Wake up, it's time to dig deeper than the learnings from just this life". Fear is simply Forgotten Eternal Aptitudes Returning. As you tap into that universal wisdom, that all-knowing-soul that you are, you may fear (as others may tell you) that you're "losing it". Yes, in this moment you are surely losing it and it's a time to celebrate that! You are realizing that the genius within is trying to improve your state by subtraction – by creating a simpler you.

As you tread bravely along this winding lane, you'll find that it soon widens out to become an expansive plain and whatever direction you choose will unwaveringly take you home. As you take each successive and courageous step, you'll lose something of "value" that you were attached to. Most of these valuables are the glittering and transient gems you took and clung to as you walked away from your home. Without these valuables you could never be happy and they may have included:
- People accepting me,
- People being acceptable,
- People being happy with me,
- People being happy around me,
- People agreeing with me,
- People being agreeable around me,
- People being predictable,
- People not being daunted or challenged by me,
- People only seeing the good/positive/happy/coping/wealthy/busy overcoat I put on each morning.
- Life being planned,
- Life being certain, or
- Life's rules being consistent.

As you begin to lose these things, as you need less "outside" things (as above) to bring you happiness, your wings of freedom stretch and you begin to soar. As your heavy needs are released, you'll fly with a lightness of knowing that the only restriction to your feelings of happiness, peace and passion is the way you choose to feel. You are no longer chained to the beliefs, moods and fears of others. You really begin to feel that "what others think of me is none of my business".

Yes, you are "losing it" and when you are told this, you'll treat it as a compliment and know you're really on the Right Road.

"So," you may ask, "if this New World is so brilliant, why aren't I there? How can I battle the fears and limitations that stop me getting there?"

Exercises
1. Write down a list of your addictions, or things that you need to make you happy. For example, cigarettes, drink, cell phone, your business, your home, others being happy, clothes, income and so on.

....
....
....
....
....
....

Which of these would you like to lose your attachment to? You can still have them – you just don't need them.

....
....
....
....
....

When do you feel most at peace?

....
....
....
....

Is there anything in 1. (above) that gives you peace?

....
....
....
....
....
....

Love Is All There Is

When something is lacking it doesn't exist. However, because we give it a name, it appears that it does exist. The name we give this non-existence is "nothing". Names for no-things create the impression that they're some-things, which they aren't.

Sorry folks, but the message is that there is no bad, hell or devil. There is only good, heaven and God, or, to put it in a word, LOVE. There is only Love and there is no opposite to Love.

You may feel that, to move forward, you first have to deal with the demons that have kept you stuck and afraid to move forward. It is a common conception that you must fight your desires, battle your ego and face your fears to overcome the obstacles along the way. You might typically do this by spending hours (or even years) in counselling, digging up past hurts and traumas, examining them, painful detail by painful detail, and then, with a huge cry of relief, laying them to rest in peace. If this is your chosen path, take it. Just know, however, that it's the most arduous, painful and uncertain (as to positive outcome) path. There are other more painless, effective and speedy ways.

The darkness you perceive as your past traumas is as the darkness in a room – simply a lack of light.

If you go into a house that's been shut up for twenty years, it becomes light the moment you open a door. The cobwebs and dust will take some time to clean out but the darkness does not say, "Hold on, I've been here for twenty years so you'll have to give me some time to get myself off these walls and ceilings. I should be gone in a month or two." The cobwebs and dust have substance and take time and effort to move. The darkness has no substance (it is a no-thing) and doesn't exist so it is simply gone when light enters. Darkness is simply a lack of light and when light enters a room, that's all we have – light. We cannot carry darkness into a light room and make it dark. We cannot carry a no-thing.

In the same way, your sadness is a no-thing. You cannot deal with, battle or conquer your sadness for you cannot overcome something that doesn't exist. If you try to fight with something that does not exist, you will always lose. Trying to obliterate something that isn't there is an exercise in futility – it can never be done, you will always lose and your counsellor will make a lot of money from you.

"So," you may ask, "how do I deal with my sadness?"

"You don't!" I reply.

But what you can do is find that which it is a lack of – happiness. Happiness is a thing, it has substance and it can be created and grown.

It is unfortunate that we have created names for all of our no-things for, in so doing, we have come to believe that these lack-of-somethings are actually somethings – things with substance – which they aren't.

The names we have given these lack-of-somethings include guilt, shame, embarrassment, loneliness, fear, sadness and all the big names given to various diseases. It would help if we were to call them by the substance that is lacking. Some examples are:

Accepted name	***Lack-of name***
Sadness	Lack-of-happiness
Guilt	Lack-of-responsibility
Loneliness	Lack-of-friendship
Lost	Lack-of-direction
Cancer	Lack-of-acceptance
Arthritis	Lack-of-control
Pain	Lack-of-pleasure
Emphysema	Lack-of-openness
Fibromyalgia	Lack-of-support

Of course, my arthritis may be lack-of-control while yours is lack-of-flexibility and my back pain may be lack-of-support while yours is lack-of-trust. You may be told what emotion your various sicknesses and pains relate to and that may or may not be true, for you. It will certainly be true for the person telling you. If it feels right, then it is; if it doesn't, then your pain may be indicating some other emotional or spiritual "lack-of". Find your own answers.

As we are unable to release things we are thinking of, it is impossible to improve the things we don't like about ourselves. To show you how this works, close your eyes for a minute and don't think of a pink elephant. Did you not think of a pink elephant? It's like the people who put pictures of fat people on their fridge, to remind them to become slimmer. It just doesn't work. Your mind will dwell on whatever you put in it – it cannot discern between "yes" and "no". If it's in your mind (even if you put it there to tell yourself what you don't want), your brilliantly effective mind will bring that thing into your life. That is why you can spend a lifetime moaning about your terrible life and you wonder why it never changes. What you verbalize (even if you don't like it) will be manifested in your life. The only way to change your life is to talk and think of things you don't have – hopefully things you do like!

Because our minds are unable to accept two opposing ideas at once, they will only "deal" with the first idea that comes along, which is the most noticeable or most painful. The loneliness hurts, you notice it, you label it and your mind grabs it. When your mind has grabbed "loneliness" it is unable to accept "friendship". You are now stuck with having a long and pointless battle with this no-thing (loneliness), which doesn't exist.

If we had no names for these things, we'd have very few (if any) problems at all. However, since we have created them, let's focus on the some-things that they are a lack of, and improve our lives.

For example, if your mind has grabbed "guilt" and you want to release it or deal with it, look at the some-thing it is a lack of, and then focus on that. If you've done something you wish you hadn't, there are two emotions you can choose from[22]. You can choose guilt, which is the lack-of (or negative) emotion that looks backwards. You cannot change the past so the emotion you've chosen here will get you nowhere, except backwards. The other emotion you could have chosen is "responsibility" (or ability to respond), which is the some-thing (positive) emotion that looks forward – "this is where I am; what can I do from here to improve things?" If you look forward, you'll move forward. Also, if you focus your mind on the some-thing emotion (the one with substance), the no-thing cannot be held in your mind and the pointless battle will cease – you'll start making progress.

As you flood the darkened rooms of your fears with the light of your

---

22   See the chapter, *Changing Your World*, on choosing emotions.

soul, there is nothing but light. As you floodlight your guilt with responsibility, all that exists is responsibility – guilt is not there and never was. As you floodlight your self-judgement and self-loathing with compassion and acceptance, all that exists is compassion and acceptance – self-judgement and self-loathing are not there and never were. As you befriend yourself you'll see that there is nothing but friendship – loneliness is not there and never was.

As you turn on these many lights in your soul you'll see that they are merely aspects of the One Light, the single light that is Love. Holding your fear, guilt, judgement, loathing, loneliness and other no-things in your hand, you might take them to the sea of love. Lowering your hands into the water, you'll see these no-things dissolve and return to that from which they came – that which has no separation but is the simple oneness from which we've all come and to which we're all returning. This journey of your fear back to the sea of love is your own journey back home – from separation and fear to the oneness of Love. In separation we give it many names and faces, but in awareness, connection and wholeness, we realise that Love is all there is.

There is a theory that you must claim it, name it and then release it. This means that you cannot move past traumas until you have truly accepted that you've had them. You cannot truly heal the scars of your rape until you accept and say that you were raped … you cannot get out of your depression until you admit to being depressed … and so on. If this belief is valid for you, then it will work.

If you believe it can be done with less pain and quicker results, you can simply focus on what you do want, rather than spending time and energy on what you don't want.

If you don't know what you do want, you might like a third, and middle, option. For most people it's easier to write a list of what they're not good at than a list of what they are good at. So, look at the things in your life you're not good at, or happy with, and find the opposite. Start a list right now and you can add to it as you think of other things.

Once you've got a list of negatives (or no-things), write beside each one the opposite. Once the two lists are done, step back and look at each item – which one(s) would you like to change right now and which ones can wait a little while? Number them in order of priority and start with number one today.

Philip J Bradbury

For example:

My life in hell   *My life in heaven*   *Priority (No.)*
(feelings I'd like to change)   *(feelings I'd like to have*

My life in hell	My life in heaven	Priority (No.)
Addicted to smoking	A non-smoker	6
Poor	Affluent	5
Sad	Happy	7
Lonely	Have good friends	2
Judged by my parents	Understood by my parents	4
Bored in my job	Inspired in my job	3
Abused in my relationship	Loved in my relationship	1
Like I'm missing out or lost	Involved and with direction	8

Exercise

My life in hell   *My life in heaven*   *Priority (No.)*
(feelings I'd like to change)   *(feelings I'd like to have*

....

....

....

....

....

....

....

....

....

....

....

....

Changing Your World

Choosing your emotions is choosing your world.

There are two ways in which you can change your world:

The first way is to change everyone else. You can try to get your children to start listening to you, your spouse to be more supportive, your boss to be more pleasant, your co-workers more helpful, all the drivers more courteous, the police more accepting of infringements, the city counsellors more imaginative, the politicians more honest, your neighbours more generous and so on. This is valid if you only come across four or five people in your lifetime for it can take a whole lifetime to change just one person. However, if there are any more people in your world, you'll just become very frustrated and embittered – no one is going to change for you. Why should they? They don't need to and they won't. The other strange phenomenon you will observe is that the more you try to change someone, the less they will. If you leave them alone, they'll magically change before your eyes!

The second way is to recognise that the world isn't going to change and you then spend your energy on changing your reaction to every one else. This is a little more manageable, for you only have one person to focus on and you have a little more control over that person, for it is you!

How do you do that?

Let us drive into Brisbane (my city) at rush hour where there is crawling, bumper-to-bumper traffic, down the two lane road. You are concentrating on the cars ahead, behind and beside you and, also, thinking about a few other things as well. Your head is full and you're focussed on getting there happily and safely. Then, suddenly, squeal of tyres, noisy engine and a car unexpectedly pushes in front of you from a side road, causing you to brake and swerve. You nearly collide with the intruder and the car behind.

The first step is that your body goes into automatic – you put the brakes on, swerve a little, check the rear vision mirror, brake again, change down, and you're safely back to normal. You've dealt with the immediate emergency at hand.

Next, your emotions come in.

Maybe you're a young dude with a hot, flashy car and you rather fancy yourself as a racing driver. In this moment, you're really proud of your amazingly quick reactions and driving skills. When you get to work, you tell all your mates how your incredible driving skills saved an accident.

If you're another person, you might flare up in anger, toot your horn, shake your fist, shout obscenities, and curse to yourself all the way to work, where you spend the day moaning about young, irresponsible drivers.

A third person might think, "Oh dear, that poor person. Perhaps they have a sick child and are desperate to go somewhere urgently. Here was I, just thinking of myself and not of others waiting for ages. If we all let someone in, we'll still all get to work …" and when you get to work, you tell a friend about how embarrassed and selfish you feel.

Same event, different reactions. Three different ranges of emotions – pride, frustration and embarrassment.

Yes, you have a choice. Emotions are not things that happen to you; they're the reactions you choose in any given moment.

"How can I have been making choices when I wasn't aware that I was making them?" you may ask. Whether you're aware of your decision-making, you've been doing it all your life and the choices you've been making are probably the ones your parents taught you – the ones they've been using, which they learned from their parents … How many times have you said, as a younger person, that you're determined not to repeat some of the less desirable behaviours of your father or mother, only to be told, several years later, "You're behaving just like your father or mother!" When we make our decisions unconsciously, we fall back to the learned ones. When we make our decisions consciously (with awareness of who we are and where we've been), we begin to really take charge of our lives. It takes practise for more appropriate (for you) choices to become a natural part of your life, just like you practised walking as a toddler.

We fall back into old behaviours because we're all looking for love – in the wrong places. Over 90% of what we do is based on a need to find love. Let's see why ...

When we arrive here, we have a dream and not much else. We come into this world as absolutely helpless bodies – we have to rely on others to feed us, move us, clean us, protect us, warm us and amuse us. We can do nothing for ourselves. These big people immediately assume god-like status (in our eyes), as our whole being and survival depends on them. We think they're wonderful.

At the start they think we're wonderful too. We can piddle into their purses, poop on their carpet, vomit on their new dresses, spit over their food, scream all night and day and they still coo over us. We can be the most obnoxious and disgusting beings imaginable and they still cuddle, feed and love us. And their friends and relations immediately like us, even when we're not putting on a performance. We may just be minding our own business, asleep, and they all think we're so beautiful. We cannot do anything wrong and it's a totally unconditional world we live in.

Then it changes. Soon, the love we're given becomes conditional. Unless we sit properly at the table, say the right words, be quiet at certain times, help with certain duties, eat certain food and be entirely pleasant and cooperative, that love is withdrawn. We'll notice a frown and immediately search for the correct love-inducing behaviour, to turn it into a smile. Then we start interacting with those of a similar age to us and, to get the love we need from them, we learn their conditions, which are often opposite from the conditions set by our parents. Then school provides a third, often conflicting, set of conditions. To get love from our teachers we must behave in certain ways. We measure their love in the test marks we get and so we strive to say and do the "right" things to get higher grades.

Then we get a job and, again, the love we're looking for from superiors and colleagues is conditional on wearing a certain uniform, using certain language and performing certain duties in a certain way – whether we agree with any of it or not. We'll put ourselves into suits that restrict our movements, into ties that choke our creativity and into skirts that make us take small steps, all to earn some of that conditional love. We may measure that love by the dollars in our pay packet and we'll compromise and prostitute ourselves in all sorts of ways to earn that love.

Then we learn the love-inducing behaviours from our spouse and our children to earn more of their conditional love ... and we wonder where the real "us" went.

Or, we may join gangs and commit crimes to earn love from our friends. And when a thief is caught, the policeman may ask, "Well, well, well. What are you looking for?" With absolute honesty, the thief will answer, "I'm looking for love." And the policeman, in performing his duties, is looking for the same thing and measuring it in the money and promotions he receives.

No one is not looking for love and all behaviour comes back to that, which is why it is so difficult to change your behaviour.

At some stage, you work this out for yourself and realise that all love is conditional on some particular behaviour from you. You're trapped in everyone else's rules and expectations. You might get frustrated, angry, depressed or sick and then, in a blinding flash of inspiration, you learn that there is a source of unconditional love – yourself! Yes, within your wondrous self, there is so much love that you could power the whole U.S. navy and have some left over for heating all of New York. You had forgotten that, all this time, there was an inexhaustible supply of love and you can get it at any time, whether you're being nice or nasty. When you begin to tap into this eternal source of unconditional love from within is when you start leaving old behaviours behind. Then, and only then, can you start becoming who you really are.

Remain conscious, from now on, of the choices and you'll soon be acting the way you want to and not feel out of control. With consciousness and control comes greater self-awareness and that, as you'll recall[23], is what you're here for.

Exercises

1. Make a list of all the emotions (good and bad) that it's possible for humans to feel. Out of this long list:

Tick or highlight the emotions you've been choosing or experiencing to date, then

Tick or highlight (in a different colour) the emotions you'd like to be

---

[23] See the chapter, *Your Life Purpose*

choosing or experiencing.

2. Sit comfortably and close your eyes. Recall an incident in which you experienced unpleasant emotions. Now, in your mind, replay the scene but, this time, change your reaction. You may like to "play" with the scene several times in your mind, creating different reactions. Observe how you feel about that incident now.

For example:

Someone had criticised something you did and you felt absolutely crushed – belittled and embarrassed. Now, in your mind, replay the scene and this time you're assertive (though not abusive) and you quietly point out that the criticism hurt you and then you point out why you did the job the way you did and that you feel you did it rather well.
Or:
In a similar incident, you had become defensive and argumentative. Now, in the replay, you thank your critic for their constructive help, you value their opinion and you'll consider ways of improving your performance.

3. Sit comfortably and close your eyes. Picture a recurring scene in your current life in which, each time you react in a way that you always regret later on. Now, replay the scene and imagine yourself acting in a way that you're proud of. Again, you may like to "play" with the scene several times and try different words and reactions. How do you feel each time you improve your reactions? When this next happens, observe whether the outcome is better.

For example:
Whenever you ask your partner to help with the dishes, they mumble and do something else. You normally find yourself having to yell and demand that they help, and you justify it by pointing out all the things you do around the house and all the things they don't do. Now, replay the scene several times and try different approaches – ones you'd be proud to use – and create a positive outcome for both of you.

Anger And Depression

Depression is anger without energy. Anger is depression with fire.

Anger and depression are two common (and opposite) ways of expressing emotions – they are not, however, the emotions themselves.

A mechanic will not just say, "Your car is noisy" – he will say, "Your car is noisy because there's a hole in your muffler" (or whatever the reason). The noise results from some inner problem in your car and mechanics are generally more honest and thorough than doctors and psychologists.

Doctors and psychologists (in general) will not look for reasons for your noise (your behaviour) and their first impulse is to find a label for your behaviour, creating the impression that they're intelligent. It saves them having to delve any further. Inept practitioners will tell you that you're suffering from depression or anger, and this is no help to you at all. What can you do with that information? Nothing! These practitioners will assume that you are as stupid as they are and that you are more interested in having labels than solutions. If you are looking for solutions, you'll want more than these people can provide – find another practitioner.

Both depression and anger come from the same source – one of many emotions – and whether you express it as depression or anger is your choice, based on your upbringing and nature. In general, men are forbidden to cry so they'll choose anger, while women are forbidden to be angry so they'll choose depression.

The anger and depression is what you see on the top of the iceberg, but that is not the iceberg. The feelings underneath can be exactly the same, but they can be expressed by different people in different ways. The same emotion can result in different behaviour from the same people, at different times.

Any of the emotions "under the water" of the iceberg can trigger anger or depression – the choice of reaction is yours, depending on your upbringing, nature and state at that moment. Whether you choose depression, anger or one of the many behaviours in between those two, is up to you.

Anger does not happen to you – you choose it as your outlet for your emotions.

Depression does not happen to you – you choose it as your outlet for your emotions.

Go beyond your behaviour to the emotions and you'll better understand your feelings and actions. So, how do you stop being depressed or angry?

Non-reaction

One way is to simply decide not to react at all. Each time you get angry or depressed, you are making a behaviour decision. So, simply decide to change it to a decision of non-reaction. When you feel an emotion rising in your body, be still, breathe deeply and allow it to rise up to the top. As it does, hold out your hand, palm upwards, and allow the emotion to land on it, gently. From there you can look at it, turn it over, examine it in detail and then toss it away, unless you want to keep it. As you allow the emotion to rise in your body there may be physical sensations like heat, coolness, tingles, tears and waves of energy. Simply allow them to happen, keep breathing deeply and don't restrict the flow of emotions by trying to stop or analyse them.

This is easy to explain and to do – eventually. Once you have chosen non-reaction you may forget every so often, in the heat of the moment. However, as you're now an expert at walking after first falling and stumbling, many years ago, you will soon become an expert at non-reaction. And, as you do, you'll begin to know yourself with incredible insight and you'll also notice that you gain a huge amount of control over your life.

This non-reaction choice does not mean that you spend the rest of your life sitting around like a jelly-fish, doing nothing. It simply means that you do not waste your energy on being controlled by your past or your environment. With this spare energy and greater control, you'll have boundless energy to direct your life in any way you choose – your effectiveness will increase many-fold. Far from being a jelly-fish, you'll become a much more dynamic, active and effective agent of positive change in your world.

Posture awareness

Another way of taking charge of your life is to become more aware of your posture. In order to get into a depressed state, you have to put on a frown, put your lower lip out, look down, hunch your shoulders, bend forward, take short, shallow breaths, let your arms flop and point your toes inward. It is hard work being in a depressed state! When you're feeling good, take the above stance and see how you feel. Depressed? So, next time you feel a depressive state coming, take on an opposite stance – relax your face, look up, smile, straighten your shoulders, stand up, take deep breaths, raise your arms and straighten your feet. Do this now and see if you can bring on a depressive state. It is almost impossible, as it is almost impossible to cry when you're looking up. Next time your child can't stop crying, lift their head up – whew! No more crying!

If anger is your favourite reactive state then you'll have to frown, tighten your jaw, glare, lean forward, take short, shallow breaths, clench your fists, raise your shoulders, tighten your stomach and stand with your legs firmly apart. When you're feeling happy, take on this stance and see how you feel – is anger rising? Now, do the opposite – relax your face, smile, breathe deeply, open your hands, relax your shoulders, raise your chest gently, stand upright and bring your legs closer together. Now, try to feel angry. You probably can't in this stance. Practise it and next time you're in a tense situation, slip into this "cool" stance and watch your positive new self deal with the situation in a completely different (and better) way.

Don't talk about anger or depression

Rather than telling others that you're angry or depressed, tell them that you're feeling lost, worried, abandoned or any of the other feeling words that you're feeling. Take anger and depression out of your vocabulary and substitute those doing words with feeling words.

Some of you will be tempted to cheat and, instead of talking of anger, will use words like mad, wild, furious, pissed off and so on.

Instead of using the depression word, you'll start talking of feeling down, moody, listless and so on.

Using a substitute for anger or depression gets you where the labels got you in the first place – nowhere! The idea is to identify why you're feeling the way you do and you'll know when you're cheating yourself. You deserve better than that.

Exercises
In a quiet place, where you have no interruptions, recall an upsetting incident which put you into a depressive state. Observe your stance. Does the depressive feeling begin to take you over? Now, change your posture and take the opposite stance, observing whether the depressive feelings change into something else.

In a quiet place, where you have no interruptions, recall an incident which put you into an angry state. Observe your stance. Does the angry feeling begin to take you over? Now, take the opposite stance and observe whether the angry feelings change into something else.

In observing your stance, certain parts of your body will give you a good indication of your feelings:
Brow – is it smooth or creased?
Eyes – what direction are they looking, are they open or shut?
Eyebrows – are they up, down, or relaxed?
Jaw – is it relaxed or taught?
Mouth – is it open or shut, are the corners pointing up or down?
Hands – are they clenched or open?
Shoulders – are they drooping or up, are they tight or relaxed?
Back – is it rounded or straight?
Chest – is it puffed out or caved in?
Knees – are they apart or together?
Feet – are your toes facing away or towards each other?
Whole body – is it upright, leaning forward or sideways?
Speech – is it loud or mumbling, is it relaxed or stuttering?

N.B. It is advisable to firstly choose mildly upsetting situations and as you get better at changing your state, you can move onto other more upsetting incidents to clear from yourself.

By doing this with the major events in your life, you can recreate your past and this will result in a new you, in the present.

So, a new past, a new present ... let's create a new future, one with your Intention firmly in mind ...

Stepping Out

We take a first tentative and very courageous step alone,
then we take the last simple step and the applause is deafening.

By now, things in your life should be getting better – you'll be starting to have a little more control of your life, people will be treating you better and the world will seem brighter.

If nothing's changed by reading this far, it's probably because you haven't been doing the exercises at the end of each chapter. The exercises are there for you to do and if you haven't been doing them, throw this book away immediately – it's absolutely worthless unless you do the exercises.

A friend told me about a colleague who rushed up to him recently, full of enthusiasm, and told him all about the latest book he was reading – it was just so amazing and could have a huge impact on his life etc. etc. When his colleague's torrent of enthusiasm subsided, my friend asked him what had happened since the previous book – another "amazing" book he had read. There was a stony silence, while his colleague tried to recall it.

As spectators, most people go through life filling their heads with "amazing" stuff from books, seminars, workshops, tapes and so on, and where does this amazing stuff go? Usually nowhere. It stays in people's heads and no one benefits from it.

If you want to get on the train to your chosen destiny, you have to be prepared to pay for the ticket – you don't get on for free. On this Life Train, you get what you pay for and if you expect a free ride, you'll get it – to nowhere!

So, what's the cost of a ticket? The cost is that you actually have to do something with the "amazing" stuff that goes into your head. As you know, you are a channel for universal energy and universal wisdom. To date, you have been absorbing a lot of it via parents, teachers, friends, books, tapes, workshops, movies and all sorts of other sources. The universe, in its own amazing way, has nourished you with whatever you have needed in every given moment. But, not only has it given you sufficient for your needs, it has given you a surplus to pass on to others.

Once you have received that energy and wisdom, it never leaves you. You may recall that many times you have received an idea from somewhere and you were going to do something with it, but you didn't in the end. So where did all those brilliant ideas go? Did they just evaporate or go poof! after their use-by date? No, they're still in that amazing container of yours (your body) awaiting expression – all of them. They didn't disappear but if you leave them for too long they will, like fruit, begin to ferment and go sour. If you deny the inspirations you receive, you can easily become bitter, disappointed, and self-blaming and spend your later years (as many do) as a wishbone – wishing you had done this, that or the next thing.

You can change the future that's being created from your procrastination, confusion and fear, by becoming a backbone – by standing up, supporting yourself and your world. This is your opportunity to make a positive difference to yourself and others. This is your opportunity to do what you originally intended to do. Your Original Intention is still patiently waiting for you to pick it up, dust it off and let it shine. No one else can do this thing. No one else can perform this little miracle. You are chosen, you have chosen and you still have choice to:

1. Leave that Original Intention trapped in your fear and indecision, or
2. Release it to give your life greater purpose and abundance and your community more joy.

You would not have created your Original Intention if it was not possible. It is entirely possible, and whether that possibility becomes probability and then reality, depends upon your choices. The choice is actually very easy to make, but carrying it out may not seem so easy. The "doing it" is what lets most people down – they just don't.

How many people do you hear saying things like:

"I'd love to be a famous opera singer",

"I really want to make beautiful and unique furniture",

"I'd like to save our forests",
"I wish I could do something to relieve poverty",
"I want to get into politics and make it more honest", or
"If only I could help rape victims in some way …"

And yet, in spite of all these strong desires, not one single step is taken towards achieving any of these things.

And that, you see, is all that needs to be done – one single step. To reforest the planet, change the face of politics or stop cruelty to animals seems impossible – it's such a huge ambition and there's only little old you. It's just too overwhelming so you don't even start. And that's as far as most people get – thinking grand dreams and not even starting. The 1% or 2% who get to the top of their chosen activity are the ones who took that first, small and apparently insignificant step.

Mahatma Gandhi's father told him that if he was going to aim for anywhere, aim for the top because there's much more room up there. He was right – it's so much easier, in the short-term, to stay at the 'bottom', wishing, hoping and praying that someone else will lift you up with a lottery ticket win, a perfect partner "just turning up", some wealthy person recognizing your talents or some other lucky event. Sorry, but the news for today is that these "lucky" events are waiting for you to take your first brave step. Only when you've shown some willingness to help yourself will "luck" step in and help you with the next step.

So the "bottom" is filled with the masses, immobilised and trapped there by the enormity of the task, unable to make even one positive move. With so many at the bottom, it's impossible to stand out. It's so much easier to stand out and make a difference at the top.

Those who do make a huge difference on this earth don't usually see the whole picture – they go from day to day and that's how they stay unaffected by the size of their destiny.

Can you imagine a four year old black boy, living in Shantytown in South Africa, with poor and uneducated parents, telling his mother that he was going to free his people, get rid of apartheid and become the Prime Minister of South Africa. He also warns his mother that he will probably have to spend about twenty-eight years in prison to achieve this. What would have been your reaction if you had been his mother? Of course this conversation didn't happen – I don't know how Nelson Mandela thought, but I'm sure he never imagined, at that age, how much he was going to accomplish.

Can you imagine a six year old girl, with poor, uneducated parents, in a small Yugoslavian village where there was constant fighting and where you were judged by your ethnic group, telling her father, "Daddy, I'm going to move to India to help feed the starving people. I'm going to teach the people of the world about compassion and being non-judgemental and I'll be asked to give international speeches and I'll get to meet and teach most world leaders. My name will be known for the rest of history." How would Mother Teresa's father have reacted if his little daughter had said that? Disbelief? The little girl would have disbelieved it too, if she was told what she was going to do and achieve.

As Abraham Lincoln said, "Thank God that the future only comes one day at a time." It is said that time is Nature's way of stopping everything happening at once and that's how you'll operate if you're going to achieve anything – one day at a time. Maybe even one minute at a time. We're also told that if you want to give God a good laugh, tell him your plans! Nobody really knows their potential and where each step will lead – all we can do is take each little step and the big picture will present itself in small manageable portions.

As you take one small step, check how it feels in your body. Do you feel excited, calm, positive, sure or whatever, when that step is taken? Or do you feel uneasy, frightened, disempowered, or some other negative feeling? As you take a step, you'll know whether the next should be in the same or a different direction. You'll never know by thinking about it. You actually have to do something physical and then, and only then, will the next step present itself.

The average American millionaire has been bankrupt 2 1/2 times – they took a step and oops! That didn't work so they know what not to do next time. Eventually, the right steps will present themselves from the wrong ones you take and, believe me, you'll take some "wrong" steps. If you haven't erred, you haven't lived. If you worry about other people judging your wrong moves, throw this book in the bin right now – if you are still living other people's lives, you'll never get to live yours, and that means discovering some interesting but wrong sidetracks. These sidetracks, or diversions, are inevitable and very necessary for although they take you away from your chosen destiny for a time they do give you a stronger sense of where you need to go.

So, as you leave a job you've hated for the last ten years, don't be critical of yourself for having wasted that time – Nelson Mandela's twenty eight years of imprisonment taught him (and many others) much about freedom.

As you leave an unhappy marriage or relationship, don't berate yourself for being a failure – you're not a failure, you're a graduate. You've learned something about yourself, we hope.

As you are able to give up an addiction, you may congratulate yourself for learning how not to waste your time and health, rather than beating yourself up for having done such stupid things.

However, if you leave a job, relationship or any other unpleasant situation and immediately begin a similar one, you may, with full justification, tell yourself off for not learning anything! We go down the wrong track to learn what the right one is. If we don't learn the lesson, we will be given it again … and again … and again … until we learn that there's another, better way. Like me in chapter 18, if we keep returning to that which does not serve us well, we'll get knocked back. Each time we return to that which is not right for us, the knocking back will be more and more painful – financially, emotionally, health-wise or in some other way. Learn the lesson and move on to something different … anything different is usually better than more of the same.

So what's your first step today …? If not now then when?

Exercises

1. Over the next week, make a list of all the things you've ever wanted to do. Keep the list with you at all times and when you remember something that comes to you, write it down. Start right now, for you're already remembering some ideas …

....

....

....

....

....

....

....

At the end of the week, review your ideas and rate them in order of your interest in doing them. Next, with the most interesting idea, write down something you can do in the next 24 hours towards achieving it. This may just mean making some inquiries about courses, starting on your curriculum vitae, writing a list of the things you want in your perfect relationship or drinking more water for your health. Just one small step. Over the next 24 hours I will commit to ...

....
....
....
....
....
....
....
....
....
....
....
....

3. Do it!

Your Favourite Program – You!

Chasing happiness is the best way to scare it away – let it come to you.

Now that you're starting to do the exercises, you're noticing positive changes – some so subtle they're hard to notice. If you've ever been sailing in a good wind and a calm sea, you might have noticed that, over the bow of the yacht (the sharp bit at the front), it is very calm and it's hard to feel much movement. However, if you turn around and look over the stern (the blunt bit at the back), the water is churned and frothy and your sense of speed suddenly increases.

As we find it hard to sense the accelerating global changes[24] because we're in them and creating them, we also find it hard to sense our own personal changes because we're in them – we're the cause and effect. A very good idea is to start a diary and don't get one with the dates already printed in it, for you'll have limited space for each day and you don't need that sort of restriction. The best thing is a lined, blank, school exercise book – it's cheaper and you create the spaces you need.

Now, instead of watching your favourite T.V. program, put that half hour aside each day to watch the most important person in your world – you! You may have to arrange this with your family and, somehow, create a sacred time and space each day that is devoted to you. This is your family's gift to you and the greatest gift to yourself – this daily ritual is worth more than all the gold in Tibet (why do you think the Chinese invaded it?) and your family and others will reap the rewards as a new you unfolds.

So what do you write? Absolutely anything and everything! First,

---

24   Per the chapter, *Whose Life Is It, Really?*

write the date and then just put down the events or thoughts as they come to mind. It may be easier to start with the events, the happenings, in your day. Then, as you're writing down the physical things, the emotional and spiritual will surface.

At first, you may have trouble expressing or explaining the feelings, but just write something, in the best way you can. No one else is ever going to read this (though it could form the basis of your first bestseller!) so the only person checking your spelling, grammar and style is you – the harshest critic you have. As you do it each day, you'll find it soon gets easier to express your thoughts and emotions with clarity, accuracy and eloquence. This will flow into the better communication you have with your family and friends. There are two other benefits:

The first is that you'll soon become aware of the subtle whispers from your body that you haven't heard before. As you do something, you'll know much more clearly whether it's right or not. Even in choosing clothes, you won't dither and struggle over what to buy – you'll just know what you like, instantly. Also, you'll find that the clothes you buy will be ones you'll be very happy to wear. Often we've chosen cars, clothes, food, computers, houses, gifts or whatever, only to find, after we've bought them, they weren't what we really wanted. This heightened awareness of what is right for you will save a lot of money and dithering time – you'll become more decisive. This heightened awareness will spill over into jobs, businesses, relationships, friendships, holidays, hobbies and all sorts of activities and situations in your life – you'll start choosing the things that are right for you and you'll feel a lot more comfortable in that new suit that is you.

The other benefit is that, as you listen to yourself and your feelings, you'll really start to appreciate and value each little moment of your magic life. You will actually hear the birds' song with more clarity, you'll notice more rainbows and you'll give and receive more smiles. This will happen whether you are writing down happy or sad things. Whatever is happening in your life, happy or sad, should be recorded in your diary, as it happens and feels to you. There will, of course, be down days and up days, but you will probably find that the next down day is not as "down" as the last down day, and the next "up" will be higher than the last. The line on your graph will not be a straight one, but its overall trend will be upwards.

Don't try to create happiness by focussing only on the positive

– happiness will come much easier if you simply observe, without attachment, and record things exactly as you perceive them. Allow your happiness to grow of its own accord – don't try to force it. In this way, it will be more permanent.

With your diary write something, every day. It might seem like a chore but if you commit to it for 2 weeks, you will grow to enjoy it and you'll actually miss it when you're in the wilderness with no pen or paper. The time you have with this person you've known for a long time and who is becoming your best friend (yes, you!), can become a life-saver, spirit-saver and the most valuable thing you can do for yourself.

If you're not a "writing sort of person" you may think that you cannot do this – as you think, so you'll be. If you're sitting there and can't think of anything to write, write down, I can't think of anything to write, or This pen just won't move, or My mind is frozen. Just stick to the facts and avoid venturing opinions about yourself, like, I was useless at writing at school, so I won't be able to do it here, or I can't write, I'm too thick. Just stick to what's happening now, not what happened in the past – you're changing, remember?

The important thing is to keep your pen moving and if it has to move through some silliness, that's fine. Keep it moving and write down whatever comes to mind, in the order that it appears in your head. There won't be any logical order (either chronologically or order of importance) to what you write and your shopping list may be interrupted by thoughts about sex, which may be followed by anxiety about your next exam, which may be followed by pondering what shoes to wear tomorrow night, which may be followed by thoughts about a friend's funeral, ten years ago. Just write as it pops into your head and when you stall, keep the pen moving by writing I've stalled.

Some days you'll only write a few lines and on other days you'll still be going after four pages. There's no upper or lower word limit and if it was a "quiet day" don't beat yourself up about it – just write, A quiet day today, weather fine and windy, heard no birds, saw no cats, saw no people, thought no thoughts, ate no food, wore no clothes, said no words, sat nowhere, stood nowhere, lay nowhere, did nothing, felt nothing, quite numb …

Each time you're finished, simply put it away, unread. Don't go back and "correct" it as it's already perfect. If you must be nosey, leave it for a week and look at it then. The idea is simply to get "head-stuff" turned into "ink-stuff".

Exercise

Go out and buy a blank, lined, school exercise book from your local stationery store, return home immediately (i.e. do no other jobs in town) sit down and write the date on the top of the first page and start writing – right now!

Just so you don't create an excuse, start writing here, now

....

....

....

....

....

....

....

....

....

....

....

....

Journey Or Destination?

Improve your score by ignoring the scoreboard.

Now, your next question: "What about all these ideas of goal-setting, creating targets and visions? If I'm just thinking day-to-day, action-to-action or even minute-by-minute, how am I going to create proper direction in my life? Surely if I am just "trying things" in my life, with some working out and some not, then my life is going to become pretty haphazard, isn't it?"

There are three things to say about your very valid concerns:
1. It's normal to fall over,
2. Enjoy your journey, and
3. Bless your addictions and compulsions.

It's normal to fall over

Firstly, look at your "straight" life, to date:
You never fell over while learning to walk,
You were always a perfect child and were never scolded,
You've always learned everything perfectly, the first time,
You never made any mistakes at school and were a top student,
You've never had your heart broken,
You've never trusted anyone you should not have,
You've always succeeded in everything you ever did at work,
You've never had a moment of sadness, bitterness or anger.

Yes, in short, your life has been absolutely perfect, faultless and you've always got what you wanted, the first time. I am right aren't I? No? I'm not? You mean you've already had some diversions and you've made some wrong turns? Welcome to the human race! Our lives are not meant to be straight lines for, if they were, we'd be learning nothing and that is your reason for being here – to find out who you really are. You can't do that in a fault-free life.

Yes, you're meant to make mistakes and if you don't, you're not alive.

Enjoy your Journey

Whenever you reach a destination (a particular job, a relationship, a sporting achievement or whatever) another one comes along to aim for … then another … and yet another …

There are many people who have focussed on their destination(s), have achieved them with amazing success and are not happy. There are many film stars, continuously mobbed by adoring fans, who feel very lonely or inadequate. There are many millionaires who feel guilty about the people they have hurt along the way or the people who are less fortunate than them. There are many people who have got down to their target weight with dieting, and still feel fat and so continue starving themselves to death. There are hundreds of thousands of "successful" people who are unhappy and the reason is that they have focused on the destination and have not learned to enjoy the journey.

If you're playing sport (say, tennis) you have an end in sight – to win. How do you try to win? Do you focus on the scoreboard? No, of course not. You focus on the ball. You focus on your technique. You observe your mistakes and try to better yourself next time. You focus on every moment and then, when it's all over, you look up at the scoreboard.

Only when you learn to fully appreciate your unique journey, with all its twists and turns, successes and failures, will you ever reach a destination with a clear head and a sigh of complete satisfaction.

Bless your addictions and compulsions

When the journey is unbearable, unpleasant or just very confusing, people will often focus more on the destination. It is as if people say to themselves, "I hate this rough road, so rather than enjoy the scenery and look for ways to avoid the holes and bumps, I'll forget the road and focus on the great feeling I'll have when I get to where I'm going." How much time do they spend on their journey and how much time do they spend arriving? Hmmm … seems to be a long time spent trying to forget the rough road. To help forget the bumpy ride, they'll create some sort of diversion or mind-numbing process that will help them to forget the road – things like smoking, drinking, gambling, shopping, being busy, cleaning, talking, visiting, taking pills, watching T.V., politics, business and countless other things to avoid the pain of the journey.

Of course, you need to shop, talk, visit, clean, make love and do these other things, but when they are done to fill an aching hole in your soul, they are not actions but activities (or busyness) – things done to avoid the pain. Some people feel powerless and, rather than see what they can learn from those feelings and grow past them, they will go into politics or business in order to fill up their power "tanks" from other people. When these activities are used for this purpose, they are avoiding pain and abusing power.

Addictions are things we need in order to feel good about ourselves – we cannot feel good about ourselves without them. Although they can be destructive to us (and we don't feel good, then!) they are the things we turn to when we are afraid of turning to ourselves.

Compulsions are the things we must do before we get on to the things that are really fulfilling and joyful for us. We need something to keep fulfilment and joy away, in order to obey the laws we've been taught:

No pain without gain,
I don't deserve …
I should always think of others,
I'm not good enough,
You don't get anything for nothing,
I'm not lovable,
Ordinary people like me don't succeed,
I'm never lucky,
I'm not special,
I'm too stupid,
I'm the one who's always left out,
I shouldn't expect too much, and/or
I always get disappointed anyway.

So, rather than focus on what a bad person you are or a bad addiction you have, look at your addiction and ask yourself why you need it. In looking under it you'll uncover your greatest needs and perhaps your greatest strengths. Like the awful people in your life, your addictions may well prove to be your greatest blessings – facing them and seeing why you have attracted them may give you the answer to the meaning of (your) life.

The road (your Life Journey) is there to be enjoyed and though it's always under construction, there's always some beautiful scenery to behold. We don't have to learn by pain and mistakes – we can also learn some things from joy and getting it "right", if we choose.

What are you choosing?

Exercises

1. Think of the six people closest to you and write a list of the compulsions and/or addictions you see in them.

2. Next to these compulsions and/or addictions, write down where their lives would be without them – what could these people be doing or feeling without these things holding them back?

3. Do 1. and 2. for yourself:

My compulsions and/or addictions	Where I would be without them
………………………………………	………………………………………
………………………………………	………………………………………
………………………………………	………………………………………
………………………………………	………………………………………
………………………………………	………………………………………
………………………………………	………………………………………
………………………………………	………………………………………
………………………………………	………………………………………
………………………………………	………………………………………
………………………………………	………………………………………

4. List the laws (e.g. on page 151) you've learned that tell you that you're settling for less. Next to each one, write the opposite "law".

Laws I've learned   Laws I'd like to live by

……………………………………|……………………………………...
……………………………………|……………………………………...
……………………………………|……………………………………...
……………………………………|……………………………………...
……………………………………|……………………………………...
……………………………………|……………………………………...
……………………………………|……………………………………...
……………………………………|……………………………………...
……………………………………|……………………………………...

The First Big Step

There is turmoil in contemplation of the first big step.
The calm starts after you take that step.

By now you're really starting to appreciate every step of your journey, every moment of every day, and the subtleties you once missed are now speaking to you quite clearly. You're realising that every person, event, illness and gift that comes to you is a reflection of something that's inside you.

When someone gets angry with you, you know there is still something to trigger anger within you. If you find people ignoring you, you might ponder who you have been ignoring – often it's yourself and the special gifts you've been hiding or ignoring. Now, you might observe and understand why women in violent relationships keep returning to them – until they learn to love themselves and respect themselves, they'll keep attracting people who don't love and respect them.

And, in the same way, we need rainbows, sunshine, bird songs, wagging tails, hugs, smiles and compliments to remind us of the love, beauty, greatness, caring and joy that's within us. Our sole purpose for being here is to find out who we really are and it's often easier to see it reflected back, rather than by looking inside.

By now, you're starting to appreciate your uncaring parents, thoughtless friends, abusive teachers and all those other people who maligned you in some way. They were showing you the pains inside yourself that needed your healing touch. And, if you ignored them, someone else would show up and reflect a worse pain … and so on until you listened and acted. You can run for a while but you cannot run away forever – you will eventually catch up with yourself.

And, not only are you becoming aware of that which is inside you (that which needs healing and nurturing, and also that which uplifts and inspires the world), you are finding ways of changing yourself – changing your stance, thoughts, words, feelings, interpretation of the world and focus. You are regaining absolute control of your life, your feelings and the people and events that come to you.

Also, with your growing awareness, you're realising that the above-mentioned (and horrible) people and events in your life could, in fact, be the greatest gifts you ever received. They pushed you far enough away from your Original Intention that you had to find your own way home. How many times did your parents tell you, "Don't climb that tree or you'll fall out and hurt yourself," and you still climbed that tree, fell out and hurt yourself! And you continue to climb more "trees" you know are injurious to your health – starting businesses, entering relationships, borrowing money, taking risks and so on – and you keep falling out and hurting yourself! Yes, history keeps repeating itself as we will never learn from the experience and mistakes of others – we have to learn and discover for ourselves. So our nasty parents, horrible teachers, lecherous bosses, spiteful friends (or whoever we see as bad for our health) push us to discover our own truth, for that is what we are looking for. We may spend many years trying to live the truths of others and, eventually, they'll become so unpalatable that we just have to strike out and find our own truth – who we really are.

It may well be dawning on you that there is a reason for every person, every event and every thought you've ever had and that you can change any of those at will. Your Original Intention will have been making itself known to you in every person, illness, accident, movie, book and feeling you experience. As you listen, watch and feel with less attachment and more attention, the whisperings of your soul will become clamours that you just can't ignore. Often, life changes are prompted by traumatic events – heart-attacks, cancer, divorce, redundancy, bankruptcy – and, as you know, some people change when they see the light and some wait till they feel the heat. How hot does it have to get before you change? That choice is yours and you know how to make that choice.

Sometimes, acting on that choice can be very difficult – leaving a marriage, giving up a job, changing your diet, changing your friends, giving away assets, moving house – and you can easily become besieged with guilt, fear, pain, tears, anger, depression, confusion and a hundred other unpleasant feelings.

It is a bit like escaping from a sinking ship. As you leap into the cold and turbulent water beside this sinking hulk, you have to struggle with every fibre of your body to resist being sucked down. You struggle and fight the grip of that mighty force and inch by inch you claw your way to safety. As you move further from the sinking ship, the waters become calmer and it is easier to swim away. As you get even further away, you can begin to relax a little for, by now, you know there is no danger of being drawn back and sucked down. At this point, you might look up for a lifeboat, a floating spar or someone who can help. As you climb into the lifeboat, you might, then, look around to see who else you could help.

It is those first few inches, first few days, first few decisions that can be the hardest. You have no energy to think of anyone else – you have to be absolutely selfish. You simply have to create enough distance, as quickly as possible, from that which you're leaving and you're in pure survival mode – just getting to your first lifeboat, or place of safety, is all you can focus on.

So, let's see if we can make those first few steps a little easier. Instead of having to leap into the surging foam, let's see if we can arrange a lifeboat right below you. Or, better still, perhaps we can lower you over the side in a lifeboat, in complete safety. This is not always possible and, sometimes we have to just make that bold leap into the dark, hoping that it will work out – as they say, you can't leap a crevasse in two short jumps. However, there are often stepping stones, or safe places, that you can create, as you make your changes.

For example, if you're giving up drinking, smoking, drugs or you're going on a diet, you might like to find a friend, mentor or counsellor who will help you stay on your new path. Probably the best is someone who has been where you are going (e.g. an ex-smoker) and someone who has achieved what you want to (they have successfully stopped smoking). So, before you start on your new way, find such a person, let them know what you plan to do and how they can be of most help to you. If they are unable or unwilling to help in the way you want them to, find someone else. Keep looking – there will be someone who can help, if you're determined enough to make your changes.

Also, it's good to let your smoking, drinking, drug-taking or eating-a-lot friends know what you plan. Their reaction will tell you whether they are "safe" to be around. If they say things like, "Just one puff won't hurt", or "A little cake won't matter", then stay away from them. You will be threatening their fears and insecurities and they won't want you to change. Find people who will help and encourage you to make those changes. As said before[25], this little change will mean a whole host of other changes and, among them, could be the people you associate with. How badly do you want to change? Part of the cost of the ticket, on this train of life, could be losing some old friends. You do know, however, that the new ones will more accurately reflect the new you. It is worth it!

Another safe space may be educating your friends. You may have a really good friend but they are prone to giving advice. You know that, apart from that trait, they will be a rock you'll need while you're going through your divorce, job change or whatever. So, before you make any drastic changes, tell this friend what you intend to do and what you would like from them. It may be that you just want them to listen, so tell them that. They may not be good at that so have a practise with them – this can be fun and enlightening for both of you. So, whatever safe space means to you, let them know what you'll need. Good friends may not be psychic but they'll want to do the best for you – tell them what that is.

Another safe space may be a physical place – in the bush, at the seaside, in a bedroom – so look around while it's calm before the storm, and find or create that safe sanctuary. Sometimes we need a place where no one else will disturb us. Maybe it's under a favourite tree (trees and the sea are really trustworthy, happy to hear and take your problems away and they're really intelligent, giving helpful answers when we listen – rocks are similar but they take a little longer to answer) or in a friend's garden or the toilet at work. Try to anticipate your likely needs – you may need a place of quiet, you may need physical exertion, you may need to scream, you may need people around – and whether it's a cave, a tree, a couch or the arms of your mother, think of the way you deal with things and find a safe place that suits your nature and your needs.

Another safe space consideration is how you behave or deal with things when it gets too much. If you've always exploded with anger,

---

25   See the chapter, *Becoming Your Parents*

you may want to think about an opposite way – simply say, "I'll think about that and come back to you", and walk to your "safe place", which may be just somewhere in your mind if you can't get there right away. Or, if you've always sulked and not talked for days, you might like to create a statement like, "I'm feeling too hurt to handle this at the moment. Let me have some space and I'll talk about it later." Search in your mind for phrases that, with courtesy to others, give you a safe space in time and, in that, you can change your posture, choice of emotions and, hence, your reaction.

If you're having arguments in a relationship that you want to improve, you might, between you, create a safe space with a word, phrase or noise that cools things when they get too hot. You might like to agree on a goofy or profound word or phrase, ring a bell or put on a particular (silly) facial expression which says, in effect, "I feel that we have gone past the point of being constructive. Let's call time out, put the issue aside, have a cup of tea and return to the issue in two hours." While you are having your cup of tea, you may like to take turns, telling each other what you like about them. What attracted you to someone is often what pulls you apart and, most probably, the issue will be linked to something in your initial attraction for that person:

The attributes that ...

attracted you when you married	*annoyed you when you divorced*
Determination	Stubbornness
Flexible, Easy-going	Indecisive
Really good to talk to	Never stops talking
Outgoing	Show-off, flirt
Sensitive	Moody
Stable	Boring
Honest	Confrontational

Put the issue aside, come back to the positive and then, when you're both ready, return to the issue – don't ever ignore it, for it won't ever ignore you.

So, while you're slightly sane and calm, try to think of the things that make it safer for you to handle life, whether you are going through change or not – it's easier than trying to think about it later, when the mayhem has started.

Exercises
1. What physical places are the most calming and restorative for you. E.g. trees, the sea, your bedroom, a cliff-top, a favourite coffee bar, etc:

....

....

....

....

....

....

....

....

2. List the attributes you would like in the people around you when you're stressed.

....

....

....

....

....

....

....

....

....

Make a list of the people you know who have these attributes.

....

....

....

....

....

....

....

....

Write down some phrases that give you space in which to return to feeling better about yourself and the situation.

....

....

....

....

....

....

....

....

My Life In Hell

Knowing what we want can be found by knowing what we don't want.

Now we're ready to create (or recall) a grander vision of where we'd like to be. Of course, your first resistance statement might be, "I haven't a clue of what I'd like to do or where I'd like to be – I just want to get out of this awful job (or marriage, unhealthy body, addiction, town or whatever)". You know what you don't want but you don't know what you do want. So let's work (play?) with that:

Write down a list of the activities, emotions, environment, people (and anything else) that you don't like about your present situation. Once you've finished your List from Hell, write beside each item, the opposite. Your list could look something like this:

Life/job/relationship in Hell	*Life/job/relationship in Heaven*
Cold, cloudy climate	Temperate or tropical climate
Commuting 2 hours each day	Working from home
Critical boss	Supportive boss
City apartment	House on a farm, in a forest
Feeling bored	Feeling inspired
Lack of direction	Feeling decisive
Violent, abusive partner	Loving, affectionate partner
Daily routine	Variety
Working on computer	Working with animals or people
Gossiping friends	Trustworthy friends
Bossy parents	Parents who listen
Feel overweight	Feel slim and fit

Painful arthritis	Pain-free body
Cigarette addiction	Smoke-free
Always short of money	Always have more than my needs

Many things will come to mind, sparked by previous things you've written down, so keep adding to the list as you think of things. There is no logic happening here – you're not trying to work out how you're going to get these great things, just saying what you'd like, so keep adding to your wish list with no thought of how you'll achieve your Life from Heaven. That comes later …

Exercise:
Complete the following for yourself …

Life/job/relationship in Hell	*Life/job/relationship in Heaven*
………………………………………	………………………………………
………………………………………	………………………………………
………………………………………	………………………………………
………………………………………	………………………………………
………………………………………	………………………………………
………………………………………	………………………………………
………………………………………	………………………………………
………………………………………	………………………………………
………………………………………	………………………………………
………………………………………	………………………………………
………………………………………	………………………………………
………………………………………	………………………………………

My Life In Heaven

The more you take from this universe, the more there is for me.

And now comes the last step – the one you may have thought should have been the first one. It's now time to look up, look out, be expansive and recall your Original Intention. If you had done this at the start, your vision may not have been purely yours – it might have been that of your parents, with shadings from your teachers, friends and society … and even something in there from you, if you were lucky! If you've been doing the exercises, the stirrings in your heart will be loud and clear and in each living moment your Original Intention will emerge from the fog of your knowing with greater clarity.

If you haven't been doing the exercises, you're still a sleep-walker – you really have no intention of actually making any changes in your life and you'll probably read another book, watch another movie, do another workshop, watch some more TV and wonder why nothing is changing. God only helps those who help themselves and if you can't commit to yourself, what's the point in being here – just to watch the world go by and wish you could be like someone else? Yes, a strong message and perhaps it's time to stop pretending; time to stop flitting across the surface of life; time to stop being a passive spectator; time to actually wake up. If that time is now, the next step is easy – simply say "YES!" to yourself and start the book again and, this time, loving yourself and your fellow earthlings enough to actually do the exercises.

The time and effort you put into your own positive development is the amount of love you have for yourself or, in other words, the amount you value yourself. At your hourly rate, what does half an hour each day cost? Are you worth it? Is the outcome worth it? Your answer is not the words you answer with but the actions you answer with. Saying, "YES!" is easy but doing "YES!" is different. Stand in front of the mirror and look into your eyes for thirty seconds and then give your answer – to yourself. If you cannot look into your own eyes for more than ten seconds, it is definitely time to read and do this book again. The length of time you are able to look in to your own eyes is a measure of your self-awareness – or self-esteem, which is the same thing.

[Self-esteem is a measure of the distance between where you think you are (what you think of yourself) and where you would like to be. The greater the distance, the less the self-esteem, or self-awareness.]

Now, if you're ready to "take off" on your new journey, you've probably already started. However, just so you don't start thinking that the repairs on your Road of Life are completed, we'll give you something unattainable to reach for.

For this exercise, you can use the journal that you've started. You can do this every year (say, on your birthday or at New Year), for your desires and dreams will change as you do. Nothing is etched in stone and you can (must?) change course every once in a while.

Before you start, remember that you have a little bag (some bags are bigger than others) on your back – a bag you've been carrying since early childhood. The bag is called your SAD bag. Since you heard your first promise, you've been disappointed many, many times. You wanted a pretty doll or a green racing car for your fourth birthday and all you got was a silly hat! You wanted to go somewhere on holiday but your parents couldn't afford it. You wanted to sit next to that hunky guy but your teacher wouldn't let you. You wanted to go to a dance with that beautiful girl but your parents wouldn't let you. You wanted that promotion but the boss's favourite got it. You wanted to have a happy family and all you've got is a divorce and two confused children. All your life you've ordered something from Universal Takeaways and they've always delivered something a little less – they've short-changed you all along. And that is where sadness comes from – you have an expectation and it isn't met. In fact, you've had so many unmet expectations, you've learned to ask for a little (or a lot) less than you really want. You've deliberately short-changed yourself in your desires so that you won't be disappointed, for disappointment hurts. Disappointment (or getting less) hurts more than expecting less – or does it? The SAD (Systems for Avoiding Disappointment) bag is getting very heavy with all your unrealised dreams filling it up. Before you start this exercise, please take the bag off, put it outside, open it up and let the undreamt dreams out. If you want to put the bag back on later, you're welcome, but if you leave it out for a day or two, it will dissolve. Your choice …

Now, in your journal (or wherever you're doing this exercise), write your name and date at the top except that the year is not this year, but the year three years from now. If today is 5th April 2016, write 5th April 2019. You have now transported yourself three years into the future. You wake on the morning of 5th April 2003 (or whatever your date is) and what you discover is that …

Write down, under the following headings, what you want your life to be like and, remember, no SAD bags – dream and imagine the grandest, most bountiful and fulfilling life you can. Do it now, and if you haven't got your diary on you, use page 168–172. Sorry, no excuses!

Surrounding environment – as you wake up and look out your window, what are you surrounded by? Is it trees, a desert, the sea, a cave, a busy city etc? Is it sunny, snowing, rainy, warm, dry etc? Is it quiet or can you hear people, music, birds or traffic? Which country is it? Close your eyes, dream and what do you experience? Write it all down.

Personal energy – as you rise, how do you feel? Are you calm, excited, peaceful, inspired, loving, centred or whatever. Write down how you'd like to feel within yourself, each day.

Surrounding people – as you wake up, who is beside you (a loving partner, no one, the cat …) and who else is in your abode – children, parents, grandparents, friends. Dream up the ideal number and type of people you'd like to live with.

Assets – as you look around on this beautiful new day, you assess your main assets – house(s), car(s), business, investments etc. List them and, beside each, write the freehold value of each of them.

Income – as you sit down to a delicious breakfast, you open an envelope that shows your income for the last year – write down the amount. Just remember that there are people currently earning over a million dollars a day so there's no need to limit yourself – nothing is impossible.

Holiday time – while munching on your breakfast, with your favourite people and creatures about you, you smile as you think of the amount of time you now have for holidays – write down the number of weeks per year that is. Remember that your work is something you're passionate about so you'll want to spend some time working! Also, if you only want four weeks a year, you may as well stay in your current job.

Pastimes – during this (now longer) time that you have for yourself (and considering your excellent income that's not dependant on you being there to earn it) there is no limit to the things you can do to amuse, inspire and expand yourself. In three years time, what can you see yourself doing? Perhaps it's travelling, workshops, bungee jumping, having time for your family and friends, having time for yourself, writing your best-seller or being pampered in some way. Write down the things you would like to be doing and be very specific about this. Don't just write travel. Write travel and then write down why you're going, who you'd like to meet, what you'd like to see and what you want to bring back from the experience. Most importantly, be very specific about what your pastimes will give you and how they will improve, amuse or enlighten you, rather than what you do in them.

Addictions – as you relax into this perfect day, you reflect on the addictions you have now released. Write down the addictions you presently have that you'd like to be free from. These may be the obvious things like cigarettes, alcohol or drugs or they may be something else you cannot possibly live without. These may be things like your business, your cell-phone, other people being happy, other people liking you or your friends. You don't have to do without any of these things – you just don't want to need them.

Worldly gifts – you came here for a purpose and, as you know, this will probably not be known in its entirety but, in this moment, write down what contribution you would like to make to create a better world. On paper, you can become the World Ruler, save all the forests, eliminate poverty and cure your mother's cancer, be a perfect mother and restore the Leaning Tower of Pisa, all at once. We're not being practical here, just imaginative. Have fun!

Worldly receipts – what will you receive for achieving one or more of your (above) goals? If you do save the forests or eliminate poverty, what will be the benefits to you in terms of physical, emotional and spiritual gains? Write down the feelings and other gains as you imagine your great work completed.

As you write these things down, you may need to continually remind yourself to take off your SAD bag again for, mysteriously, you may find yourself carrying it from time to time. Write down what you'd like and, each time ask yourself, "Is this what I'd really, really like?" Cross out what you've written and put down your true desires. You will know what you really want but you could be afraid to ask for it.

One reason for this ATAFI (afraid to ask for it) is the training you've had in NETGA (not enough to go around). There is a strange belief, in our world, that everything is limited and that's why we invented governments and rules – to allocate these scarce resources. Governments will not need to exist if we return to the reality that there is absolute abundance in this world. If the people who earned $1 million a day doubled their incomes, there would be no less for you. If you had three beach houses, instead of the one you have now, I could still have my two. If you have ultimate fame I will be no less famous. You give nothing to anyone when you deny yourself. In fact, you give a lot more when you receive a lot more. We can have it all, so go back and revise your list – be extravagant, be crazy, be totally self-indulgent for, as you know, having more of what you want gives you greater joy and fulfilment. As your joy and fulfilment increases, it spreads to the rest of us. Your feelings about yourself spread to your partner, family, friends, colleagues and to their partners, families, friends and colleagues – as the ripples in a pond, they continue spreading to the end of your universe. I'm in that universe of yours and I'd prefer that your ripples were joyful and fulfilled, rather than frustrated and limited. Sacrifice limits all of us and self-fulfilment gives fulfilment to all of us.

So now that you've completed the last exercise in this book, what do you do with it? Well, not much at all. Ask for what you want, in your grander future, let it go, and refocus on the now, revelling in every magic moment, person, smell, feeling, sight, sound and event.

You don't have to do any of this alone – you are part of a team of people who are all going the same way. Many in this team you'll never meet but, seen or unseen, they're there, working for you. And you're working for them. So, allow them the opportunity to help you, as you enjoy helping others. Receiving and accepting graciously are the hardest things we have to learn. Try it!

If you've done the exercises in this book, it means that you're prepared to do the work, to pay for the ticket, and to play your part – your team-mates welcome that commitment and are now eager to help you realise your dreams.

If you haven't done the exercises, you're not ready to join your team yet and you'll have to achieve your dreams the hard way – alone.

As you hold your vision, palm upwards, without letting it drop, you allow it to fly with help from your team-mates. Don't take from them the joy of creating some magic in the way your dreams come to you. Get out of your own way and watch the magic happen. As said before, if you want to give God a good laugh, tell him your plans. Hold lightly to your dreams and visions, always supporting them, and they'll surely come true.

How they come true may not be in the way you imagined, so allow your team-mates to work their magic and bring you the most beautiful surprises in the form of opportunities, chance meetings and unexpected BFI's (Blinding Flashes of Inspiration).

If you're focusing on the now, on the beauty and power in every moment, you'll recognise these beautiful surprises for what they are. If you've done the exercises, you'll take each golden opportunity and you'll actually do something with it. You won't waste a single one of them. Your dream and our dreams will be realised.

It was a great pleasure to have met you and I hope we meet again. Our next meeting may be in another book of mine or through one of my courses. But, who knows, our next meeting may be through one of your books, courses, songs, movies or other beautiful creations. To meet you through one of your realised dreams would be the ultimate blessing you could bestow on me. That, I await with eager anticipation.

From the explanations on pages 164 to 166, complete the following:
Surrounding environment

....

....

....

....

....

....
....
....
....
....
....
....
....
....
....
....
....

Personal energy

....
....
....
....
....
....
....
....

Surrounding people

....
....
....
....
....
....
....
....
....
....

Assets

....
....
....
....
....
....
....
....

Income ....

Holiday time

....
....
....
....
....
....

Pastimes

....
....
....
....
....
....

Addictions

....
....
....
....
....

Worldly gifts

....
....
....
....
....
....
....
....

Worldly receipts

....
....
....
....
....
....
....
....

Your new life doesn't stop when you shut this book - you might like to continue creating some joy and fulfilment for yourself and others. Here are some ideas on the next page, and you might like to add a few of your own:

Birthday Gift

A. Each birthday, give yourself the gift of friendship – take four days off, by yourself, somewhere special, do all the exercises in this book again and have fun (in other ways) with the best friend you've ever known.

B. During the rest of the year, commit the following senseless acts of kindness and random acts of love, as often as you like:
1. Ask a policeman the directions to Heaven.
2. Buy an ice cream and give it to someone.
3. Pay for two or three cars behind you, at the tollgates.
4. Ring your parents and thank them for some specific deed they did, many years ago.
5. Ring friends and say you hope they have a really special birthday, months before their birthday.
6. Stop in the street and hug yourself luxuriously, languorously and lovingly.
7. Send pressed flowers with your tax returns.
8. Pick flowers and give them to your bank teller.
9. Touch people gently when you are talking to them.
10. Send a happy picture to a politician who is having a hard time, whether or not you like him or her – the postage is free!
11. Look in the mirror and tell the person something complimentary.
12. See how many smiles per hour you can give away – ones that pop up on other people's faces.
13. Thank your children for making a difference in your world.
14. Invite your neighbours over for a bring-your-own Sunday lunch.

15. Pat yourself on the back when you do something well and say, "Thank you for excelling."
16. Pat yourself on the back when you do something badly and say, "Thank you for learning."
17. Plan a really special day with your family in your bedroom – see how many fun and interesting things you can all do in one room.
18. Write love letters to yourself, post them and keep them to read when you're up, down or in between.

Ideas To Try

Radionics

This is the fancy word for using a pendulum or for using any other tool for divining for anything – water, oil, precious metals or answers to life's questions.

A pendulum can be made of any piece of string or light chain (e.g. necklace) with a small weight attached to the end. Some people like to use a pendant and this is O.K. but any other similar thing (e.g. string and washer) will do.

Hold the pendulum in the most comfortable hand, string between thumb and index finger, elbow on a stable surface, arm at 45o and weight hanging about 5–6 inches (130–150 mm) below your thumb. Start with the pendulum absolutely still, relax your mind and body (with your arm very still) and ask (in your mind) the pendulum for a "yes". It will slowly start to move of its own accord in a certain pattern - e.g. back and forth, sideways, in a clockwise or anti-clockwise circle. If you're a bit cynical, you can stop the pendulum and ask the same question – watch it return to the same pattern.

Now ask it for a "no" and then a "cannot answer" pattern. Everyone is different and a "no" pattern for you may be a "yes" pattern for me. However, once you have found your patterns, they won't change, though you cynics may like to check every now and then!

All you now do is to ask the pendulum "yes" and "no" questions and see what it says. In doing this, please remember several things:
- The more unattached you are to the answer, the better it will work. If your question is "will this person sleep with me tonight?" or "will I get a pay rise tomorrow?" you will probably get a "yes" as your conscious mind will affect the result.

- The idea is to get your conscious mind out of the way and allow the answers to come from your super-conscious mind. If you're continually getting "cannot answer" then it may be you're getting in the way. Stop trying to predict or force an answer.
- "Cannot answer" can come up if the question is not a "yes or no" one, if the answer depends on factors not being asked about, or the question is not in the best interests of everyone.
- The pendulum may not work at all if you're feeling depressed, angry or negative in some way. You can still use it at these times but you have to put your negative feelings aside as they will block the flow of answers.

Some people have some other rules, which you can make up your own mind about:
- You should not use another person's pendulum. To me it's a tool like a broom or a hammer and as long as you ask first, don't damage it and return it, I cannot see a problem.
- If you use a new (or some other person's) pendulum, you should first ask the pendulum if you can use it. I just check the "yes" and "no" pattern and if they work for me as usual, then it's O.K.
- Don't let children under 13 years use one. I cannot see any reason why not - it's fun, harmless and if we can show our children some of the power and knowing they have, then go for it!

Ambidextrous Writing

This is used to explore various sub-personalities through two-handed writing. Your main hand is the one you usually use for writing – if you're right handed, your main hand is your right hand and your other hand is your left. Your main hand is the "facilitator" and your other hand is the "client".

Create two columns on paper and your right hand writes in the right column and your left hand in the left column.

You ask questions with your main (facilitator) hand and answer with your other (client) hand. Your client will probably write in a scrawl but this doesn't matter, just let the writing flow – it is the message that's important.

When you write a question with your main hand, the first thought (response) is the correct one to write with your other hand. Sometimes the answers may seem illogical or silly but just put down what first comes to mind. Sometimes the answers may seem like silly "mind chatter" and sometimes they may be very profound and surprisingly helpful. Just keep asking and responding, without judgement, and let the first thoughts flow onto the paper.

It is vital you don't try to consciously guide or demand a particular response. If there is no response to a particular question you may be trying too hard – this is one of those nice jobs in life where the lazier we are, the better it gets done. Just relax your body and mind, become a hollow bamboo through which the whispers of your subconscious speak, and try again.

If still no response arrives or you are getting frustrated, write that down as a response (e.g. "No response", "I'm getting frustrated", "Stupid mind, can't think!" or whatever) and ask the next question. Keep the process moving. That you are stuck or frustrated are, in fact, valid answers and can tell you much, if looked at later, with all the other responses you had.

The Alphabet Game

If you want to feel a little better at any time, simply go through the alphabet, one letter at a time, in your mind. As you get to each letter, think of a positive word that starts with it. This can be done at any time (standing in a queue, driving, at a meeting, vacuuming) and you might be amazed at how it helps.

Vision Book

Start a scrap book to put into words and pictures the things you want to do. This can be used for health, relationships, work, hobbies and any other area of your life.

For example, if you want to travel to Peru, find some pictures of the plane/ship you want to go on, some pictures of the places you want to visit and stick them into your book, with pictures (photos or drawings) of yourself with them, as if you had already been. Write out your itinerary and why you want to go. If it is for enjoyment, write the word "enjoyment" in large letters and list the fun things you want to do. If you want to go there to learn things, list them.

If you want a Ferrari Dino car, paste a picture of the car, with you in or beside it, and list the things you want included, including the price you will pay.

Just be as imaginative as you can, put in as much detail as you can and don't forget to put dates of when you want those things.

One last thing is important – blank space called "opportunity". What you are asking for in your words and pictures is the minimum and you are happy to get any "extras" you had not thought of. This "opportunity space" gives the universe the opportunity to give you some nice extra surprises.

Philip's Rejuvinated Life

Once upon a time I had it all: A beautiful, intelligent and supportive wife, who had a well-paid professional job, two happy, healthy and intelligent children, a five-bedroom house, two cars, A good income, a high status job, overseas holidays, a financially secure future …

However, unlike other fairy stories, it didn't end "happily ever after". Well, not straight away. At the precise moment of realising my good fortune, I let it fall through my fingers and walked away, feeling sad, confused, angry, frightened and very free.

My ex-wife and I had worked hard together for eighteen years, forgoing luxuries and many necessities, to create a bountiful harvest of prosperity in our future. As we looked about and started to recognise and reap that well-deserved harvest, I looked inside (for the first time) and saw a huge emptiness that could never be filled with wealth and toys. As I said to my ex-wife at the time, it felt like this huge, invisible hand was pushing me away from her and I couldn't resist its force. This yearning emptiness would not wait and I had to heed it.

At the time I felt that I had no choice – this need to fill the gaping hole in my soul was so persistent and demanding. And even if I had known how much harder it would become, I still would have left. And even if I had known how hard it would become for my children, I still would have left. And even if I had known that my father would verbally abuse me and that my parents would cut all communication with me for eighteen months, I still would have left. The crying and emptiness in my soul was such that I still cannot think of anything that could have stopped me leaving my family and adding to the suffering of us all, for a time. I didn't know about souls and feelings at the time and it's only now that I am able to form words to explain what happened then. I had no words then and only knew that I must go. Where or why I was to go I didn't know – I just knew I must obey this unseen hand.

I suppose I could have continued to pretend that I was O.K., as I had for most of my life, but I know that the pretending would have got harder and, in my constantly-conflicted state, I would have become a more angry, depressed and/or dysfunctional human.

There came a time when the pain of pretending was greater than the fear of facing my truth.

There is suffering in both inaction and in action.

There is pain pretending and in hiding behind the façade I wanted the world to see, and there is pain in ripping it off and discovering the real me. The difference is that the pain of pretence lasts as long as the pretence, while the pain of becoming real is temporary – it only lasts while we adjust to the changes we decide to make. It's like a plaster that is uncomfortable but is necessary to protect our broken leg; once the leg is mended the plaster can come off. The small pain of adjustment is certainly less than the pain of wearing it for the rest of our lives.

I cannot pretend that my suffering didn't affect others – I can still see those three tear-filled faces as I drove away that day and I can never pretend I wasn't the cause of their pain. I have been less of a father than I would have hoped. I admire the way my children have coped over the years, and I celebrate the fact that we are now becoming closer to one another.

What I'll never know is the suffering that would have been if I'd stayed and grown more embittered, lonely and separate from who I am. As I make choices, there are things I'll never know. But, in looking back, I know that I made the right choices for me. My suffering has ceased and the Philip I've come to know has become my best friend, enabling me to become a good friend to everyone else.

I left, not knowing why, where to go or what to do. I stumbled without compass or rudder and it took a long time to come to terms with the guilt, sadness and other pains. I continually wished for a wise mentor but they never turned up and so I had to turn to me – something I had never done before. The only thing that guided me was a whisper from my heart. I didn't always listen but when I did, things happened.

As I sat in my aloneness I cried my tears of pain, regret, guilt, loneliness and fear, and I withdrew from the world as my old world withdrew from me. There were only two people I could talk to – myself and my God. I never stopped nagging these two people and as I yelled at them, pleaded with them, swore at them, forgave them, laughed with them and thanked them, I came to know the best two friends I'd ever known. As I pleaded and asked my questions, I began to hear their answers. And with their answers came opportunities.

I asked why I'd spent the last twenty years in a job I'd hated. A month later I was offered a new opportunity which I took – being a lecturer terrified me but I was exhilarated and alive!

I asked about my aloneness and new friends turned up – I met new people, interesting people, interested people, my people, people I never knew existed. They had no interest in my bank account, profession or assets – they simply asked me about my feelings. It was a strange new world and I was confused and delighted. I didn't know about feelings and I started to learn from these people.

They say that if you kill a fly, all the family turns up for the funeral – the more you kill, the more there are around! Change is like that – change begets change, and as I made one change I was drawn to make another, an another, and another … I now have a different wife, a different job, a different relationship with my parents, different beliefs, different clothes, different interests, a different world … and all of these differents are also betters. Maybe my suffering was necessary so that I could learn about not suffering. Who knows?

In looking back at the changes I've made, I've realised that I'm a very slow learner and that I probably did everything in the most inept and painful way possible. I determined that my learning should be shared with others so that their path from suffering to joy would be easier and more effective and so I run the *Free To Be Me!* courses, I give talks and I write books, for in my slow and painful way of learning I've realised that I don't have to put up with the way things are – I am actually in control and I can change the nature of my relationships, my jobs, my thinking and my environment … and so can you.

About the Author

In New Zealand I experienced life as an accountant, credit manager, company director, shepherd, scrub-cutter, tree pruner, freezing worker, plastics factory worker, saxophonist, army driver, tour bus driver, stage and television actor and singer, builder, lecturer, facilitator for men's groups, reporter, columnist, magazine editor, publisher, writer ...

In South Africa as an AIDS workshop co-facilitator ...

In the Australian bush as a barman, horse and camel trekker and stock-whip teacher ...

In England as a contract accountant, corporate trainer, estate manager, lecturer, singer/songwriter, website editor/writer and freelance writer …

Now that I'm back in Australia, house renovating, teaching and writing, I'm wondering what's next!

The constant for my wife and I is *A Course in Miracles*, a psychological life-style course in forgiveness. Through it I have found the peace I had always been searching for - the journey to where we have always been.

Philip J Bradbury in social media
Website: www.philipjbradbury.com
About Me: https://about.me/philipbradbury
Amazon: amzn.to/25X0CLb
Facebook:
https://www.facebook.com/AuthorPhilipJBradbury/
Google+: http://bit.ly/2bsbpUy
Linked In - http://bit.ly/2aTzZMS
Pininterest: https://au.pinterest.com/bradburywords/
Smashwords: http://bit.ly/2aNjkic
Twitter: https://twitter.com/PhilipJBradbury
Wordpress blogs:
https://flashfictionfanatic.wordpress.com/
https://pjbradbury.wordpress.com/

Thanks

I am able to put intangible ideas into words and Anna, my wife, is able to put them into action; the reason she's such a good life coach. She is my best friend and greatest inspiration and I thank her from the bottom of my beating heart for being there, for loving me and for being that which I wish for myself. Anna edited this book with her razor eye for the details I didn't see. Thank you for seeing that which I cannot ... on so many levels. I'd like to thank a lot of people who really annoy me. As a young man I learned that "real men" are those who are capable of doing everything themselves – cooperation and asking for help were ideas for "soft men". Working with other people has been one of my hardest lessons and one of the most expansive and freeing lessons as well. Originally, being too shy to publish anything of my own, I started publishing the words of other people and I tried to do everything myself – editing, design, marketing, accounting, etc – and it was a dismal failure. Then, with some encouragement and a little more confidence, I started publishing my own words – this time I did all of the above things as well as the writing. Now, I was doing absolutely everything, except the printing and binding. Still a dismal failure.

Being too shy to show my work to other publishers[26], I initially self-published and though I sold a few books that way, I realised that "a few" wouldn't keep me in the style I'd like to become accustomed to. I eventually sent three of my books off to ten New Zealand publishers. Nine of them said, "No thanks" and one said, "Yes!" The tenth did nothing in the end but they suggested that I combine the two smaller books and their confidence gave me a boost.

And my thanks to Ursus Schwarz, a Swiss friend and a part-time New Zealander, who suggested that I include my own story in the book. This really annoyed me as it meant another week or so of rewriting but, as soon as he mentioned it, I knew it was totally appropriate – this is not an academic treatise but a book for real people in real-life situations and it is important that you know it's written by a real person with real challenges, frailties, abilities, failures and successes.

<u>The day after</u> I finally admitted to myself that my artistic talent

[26] For a while I was too shy to show my books to book stores! I soon realised I'd have to get over that shyness (or change my occupation) in order to pay for rent, food and other necessities.

did not extend to well-presented book covers, I bumped into a friend, Janne Perry, who offered to "do something". Her brilliance is self-evident and thanks, Janne.

I have a lot of other friends and to name some would be unfair to all the others so, for your support, suggestions, cynicism, enthusiasm and ideas, I thank you all.

Also, to the many *Freedom To Be You!* workshop attendees, thank you for everything I have learned from you – I chose to be a teacher to learn and in running the workshops I realise just how much wisdom, beauty and strength there is in every human being.

And, lastly, thank you to those of you who I never see but who provide the inspiration, insights and ideas that come at unexpected moments. Through you (whoever you are) I realise the small part that I play in this whole process and I also realise the huge store of knowing that we can all tap into.

More books by Philip J Bradbury

Non-Fiction
The Lawless Way
Change Your Life, Change Your World
The Twelve Week Miracle (with Anna Bradbury)
Understanding Men
Articles of Faith
Conversations on Your Business
Stepping Out Of Debt and Into Financial Freedom

Some-Fiction
Dactionary – the dictionary with attitude
The Meaning of Larf
53 SMILES
97 SMILES
45 Moments With Men

Fiction
The Royal Bank of Stories
Circles of Gold
Gerald the Great of Gorokoland

Words in progress - looking for a publisher
40 Moments With Writing
50 Moments With Fables
55 Moments With God
42 Moments With Men
22 Moments With Odes
65 Moments With Self
The Last Accusation
The Last Rejection

For more information on these books, see
   www.philipjbradbury.com

Getting your mind and life back on track ... after leaving behind expectations and oughtism

Philip J Bradbury

Published by   The Write Site, Brisbane, Australia

Copyright 2017 © Philip J Bradbury

Cover: Philip J Bradbury
Inside images: Philip J Bradbury
Book design: Philip J Bradbury

Philip J Bradbury has asserted his right under the Copyright, Designs and Patents Act 1988 to be identified as the author.

ISBN- 978-0-9954398-3-2

All rights reserved. No part of this publication may be reproduced or transmitted in any form or by any means, electronic or mechanical, including photocopying, recording or any information storage and retrieval system, without permission in writing from the publisher.

www.ingramcontent.com/pod-product-compliance
Lightning Source LLC
Chambersburg PA
CBHW050537300426
44113CB00012B/2147